THE UNIVERSITY AND THE
URBAN CRISIS

THE COMMUNITY PSYCHOLOGY SERIES
SPONSORED BY
DIVISION 27 OF THE AMERICAN PSYCHOLOGICAL ASSOCIATION
SERIES EDITOR, DANIEL ADELSON, PH.D.

The Community Psychology Series has as its central purpose the building of philosophic, theoretical, scientific, and empirical foundations for action research in the community and in its subsystems, and for education and training for such action research.

As a publication of the Division of Community Psychology, the series is particularly concerned with the development of community psychology as a sub-area of psychology. In general, it emphasizes the application and integration of theories and findings from other areas of psychology, and in particular the development of community psychology methods, theories, and principles, as these stem from actual community research and practice.

TITLES IN THE COMMUNITY PSYCHOLOGY SERIES

Volume 1: Man as the Measure: The Crossroads, edited by Daniel Adelson

Volume 2: The University and the Urban Crisis, edited by Howard E. Mitchell

Volume 3: Psychological Stress in the Campus Community: Theory, Research and Action, edited by Bernard L. Bloom

THE UNIVERSITY AND THE URBAN CRISIS

Community Psychology Series, Volume 2
American Psychological Association, Division 27

edited by

Howard E. Mitchell
Human Resources Center
University of Pennsylvania

Daniel Adelson, Series Editor
University of California, San Francisco

Behavioral Publications
New York

Library of Congress Catalog Number 74–6113
ISBN: 0–87705–139–9
Copyright © 1974 by Behavioral Publications, Inc.

BEHAVIORAL PUBLICATIONS, INC.
72 Fifth Avenue
New York, New York 10011

Printed in the United States of America
456789   987654321

Library of Congress Cataloging in Publication Data

Mitchell, Howard Estill, 1921–
   The university and the urban crisis.

   (American Psychological Association.   Division 27.
Community psychology series, issue 2)
   1. Community and college—Addresses, essays, lectures. I. Title. II.
Series: Community psychology series, issue 2.
LC237.M57   378.1'03   74-6113

Contributors

WARREN G. BENNIS, President, University of Cincinnati

EDWARD E. CAHILL, Ph.D., Research Associate, The Institute for Behavioral Research, The University of Georgia

JOHN R. COLEMAN, President, Haverford College

FRANK J. CORBETT, Director, Office of Urban Affairs and Professor, School of Social Policy and Community Services, State University of New York at Buffalo

LEONARD J. DUHL, M.D., Professor of Urban Social Policy, University of California, Berkeley and Professor of Psychiatry, University of California Medical Center, San Francisco

I. IRA GOLDENBERG, Ph.D., Harvard University

MARTHA LAVELL, Research Associate, Human Resources Center, University of Pennsylvania

MURRAY LEVINE, Professor, State University of New York at Buffalo

HOWARD E. MITCHELL, Ph.D., 1907 Foundation Professor of Urbanism and Human Resources and

Director, Human Resources Center, University of Pennsylvania

HERMAN NIEBUHR, JR., Ph.D., Associate Vice President for Urban Affairs, Temple University

YVONNE SCRUGGS PERRY, Research Associate and Coordinator of Field Services, Human Resources Center, University of Pennsylvania

PATRICIA L. ROSENBAUM, Research Associate, Human Resources Center, University of Pennsylvania

PAUL E. WEHR, Director, Center for Nonviolent Conflict Resolution, Haverford College

Contents

Foreword

The ideal of self-government, of a *universitas magistrorum et scholarium* "a guild or union of masters and students organized for mutual protection" (*Encyclopedia Brittanica*) informs the idea of the university, much as the ideal of self-government, of a participatory citizenship, informs the idea of the city (civitas, cite, city). In the United States we have had the further ideals of universal education, which at the elementary and high school levels is mandatory, and universal suffrage. But these ideals are far from the reality. And as in the ancient city-states of Greece—where those who did not enjoy citizenship were labeled barbarians—so even in our times, for even if most carry the label of "citizen," social and other conditions keep many of us alienated in spirit, attitudes, and behavior, or we continue to label others alien and barbarian on the basis of their ethnic origins, their religion, or their sex, and make it difficult for them to gain entrance into institutions of higher learning as well as other social and community institutions.

But the word citizen is a revolutionary word, and whether citizens of the City or the University, the major thrust has been towards the actualization of the meaning of this word.

If "city air makes free," in the transactional relation between the City and the University, the University has played a major role in developing a scientific-humanistic base for this freedom, even though it has at times also failed to keep pace with developments in the larger community, as happened, for example, in 19th century Oxford and Cambridge.[1]

[1]See S. Rothblatt's *The Revolution of the Dons,* London and New York, 1968.

9

In the U.S.A., further, it may be suggested that a new stage was reached in the relationship between the University and the City, in that the University became a conscious instrument of democratization, and even as America opened its doors to the poor from abroad, so the University moved toward increasingly opening its doors to previously excluded segments of the population, not without deep conflict, however, a conflict made more difficult by conditions both at home and abroad.

In America, also, the University and especially the great state universities, played a key role in fostering and developing agriculture and industry in the communities surrounding them and in the states which established them. It had, however, in the past, not been particularly concerned with specific segments of the population—women and minority groups, for example, if open to the community's youth on a differential basis. It is only in more recent times that such deprived or disadvantaged groups have been special objects of university attention, though to be sure some universities and colleges accepted only women or only members of minority groups.

In this volume, Howard E. Mitchell has brought together a group of psychologists who focus particularly on the Philadelphia story, but to them he has added a group with significant experiences in other centers of higher learning. These authors touch on many aspects of the University-City interrelationship. What a number—including Howard Mitchell—stress is the scholarly base of work in the community. The scientific-scholarly if critical approach of the University guided by the central ideal of participatory self-government may be the most revolutionary approach in providing a base not only for university reconstruction and growth but for city and citizen reconstruction and growth.

Daniel Adelson
Series Editor

Preface

Samuel C. Jackson, while serving as Assistant Secretary for Community Planning and Management, U.S. Department of Housing and Urban Development, raised a telling question in the title of his remarks addressed to the Annual Meeting of the Council of University Institutes of Urban Affairs on April 7, 1972, in Dallas, Texas. Mr. Jackson's remarks were entitled "Is the University Superfluous in the Urban Crisis?"[1]

Although the author's ultimate response to the question he poses is "no," he seizes the opportunity to point out that some universities and many academicians seem to think that it is not the business of the university to involve itself directly in the problems of the city. Indeed, social scientists such as Daniel P. Moynihan and Edward Banfield, close to the seats of power in recent years, feel that the "urban crisis" is exaggerated and they point to a reduction in substandard housing and a decline in the percentage of citizens officially classified as impoverished. Mr. Jackson counters with such facts as:

> —At least 100,000 housing units have been abandoned in New York City. ...
> —There is tangible evidence of a widening gap between the rich and the poor. According to economists at MIT, the income gap between the poorest one-fifth and the richest one-fifth has nearly doubled during the past 20 years.

[1]HUD News, U.S. Department of Housing and Urban Development.

11

—There seems no real improvement in the polarization of the races in urban regions. The proportion of blacks in the suburbs, which was five percent in 1960, was still only five percent in 1970, although the black population of the inner city rose from 16 to 21 percent.

—The urban ghettos still fester with unfulfilled aspirations fanned by hopelessness and frustration.

The contributors to Volume II of the Community Psychology Series are all university-based personnel who feel that the "urban crisis" does exist and poses a challenge for our universities. Some of these authors are psychologists and some are not. Some of the psychologists, like Murray Levine and Ira Goldenberg, are directly involved in the training of psychologists. Others, like Warren G. Bennis and Herman Niebuhr, present their viewpoints from the highest levels of university administration.

The authors, regardless of discipline or present status and role in their respective institutions, also reflect a bias in that they do not feel the time has come to retreat in the battle for equality and human resource development. If advance warnings prove correct, we shall witness during the years of the second Nixon administration the extent to which the "bandwagon effect" is operative as psychologists and their academic cohorts resign themselves and move to other problems and training areas with anticipated reductions in federal support of human service programs and training.

It is hoped that the value of Volume II for those directly engaged in the development and training of community psychologists will be a greater appreciation of how constructive action within the university related to the urban condition may assist in the development of "a viable theory of community psychology and/or a better definition of community psychology." Edwin I. Megargee, a member of the editorial board of the Division of Community

Psychology, provided this insight after reviewing the contributions of the authors to Volume II.

Warren G. Bennis sets the tone for Volume II in the presentation of his Inaugural Address at the University of Cincinnati, November 5, 1971. He perceives the University of Cincinnati as linked in a collaborative relationship with the larger community. "So many universities now survive in a situation of debilitating hostility with the communities that surround them. Our relationship with the Community is one of affection and mutual respect, and from that we both reap enormous benefits." Bennis proceeded to make one of his initial administrative acts the establishment of the office of Vice President of Urban Affairs, to assure the interdependence between the University of Cincinnati and the city.

The format for Volume II then invites the reader to focus upon Philadelphia. Following an overview in which it is explained that this is not the complete "Philadelphia Story" of the university at the service of society, a series of illustrative experiences of university-community interactions is presented. The examples cited represent psychologists and representatives of other disciplines, operating from large and small institutions, some in the heart of the inner-city crisis and others located on the suburban fringe of the Philadelphia scene. In the Points and Counterpoints section of Volume II, those unfamiliar with demographic changes in population and those who have little factual knowledge about institutions of higher learning in the Philadelphia region are provided some descriptive information.

Following the "Philadelphia Story," reports are provided by psychologists at work in other communities. Two former associates of Seymour B. Sarason, who pioneered with him in the development of the Psycho-Educational Clinic at Yale, now speak to us from their more recent endeavors in Buffalo and Cambridge. The serious reader in this area of activity and its relevance to community psychology, will more fully appreciate their message by referring to their earlier work with Sarason, Cherlin, and Bennett.[2]

The final article is by Leonard J. Duhl, a social psychiatrist with wide experience in diverse areas of public service in the policy-making echelon of the Peace Corps and HUD before going to Berkeley. Duhl provides us with an intensely personal document which, in this writer's opinion, speaks uniquely about coping behavior required at Berkeley, which may not characterize the atmosphere at more conservative colleges and universities. The extent to which this observation is true suggests that readers refresh themselves relative to insights provided in Volume I of the Community Psychology Series, which had its principal contributors located at Berkeley.

Although Duhl's paper is not as analytical as some of the others, it serves as a like companion to the lead-in article by Bennis, in its emotional tone and punch. Since no one to this author's knowledge has yet produced an adequate model of university-community relations, much of what is done must proceed empirically, based upon mutually held faith and sound clinical judgment until viable intervention theories are developed and tested. Psychologists operative in clinical areas, action-research, and the more recent domains of community psychology, are familiar with this approach as represented in Duhl's paper.

There is probably no better response to the question posed at the beginning of this Preface, in Samuel C. Jackson's speech, than to call attention to the fact that The Carnegie Commission on Higher Education published in December, 1972 a report entitled *The Campus and the City.*[3] We appropriately quote from its recommendations. The Commission viewed the relationship between

[2]Sarason, Seymour B., *et al. Psychology in Community Settings: Clinical, Educational, Vocational, Social Aspects.* New York: John Wiley & Sons, 1966.
[3]McGraw-Hill Book Co., 1972.

city and campus as not a "single relationship between two clearly defined entities but rather a whole series of relationships with the identity of the participants shifting somewhat from one relationship to another, and from time to time." They went on to say:

> that certain of these relationships carry obligations which higher education has not adequately met and opportunities it has not yet fully realized.
>
> —Increasing demand for higher education and the development of new educational clienteles with large concentrations in our cities are sometimes poorly matched by the existing higher education resources in many of our cities.
> —Shifts in the structure of jobs in professions, social services, and government provide new opportunities for joint participation in the development of revised educational programs for new manpower needs.
> —Wise choice of urban public service activities and research projects could make the city a highly effective laboratory for higher education while at the same time making positive contributions to the life of the city.
> —Ways must be found to facilitate appropriate use of higher education resources by the urban student.
> —Cities' higher education resources must be organized in a way which will enhance their overall value to the city.
> —Each college and university must learn to assess its impacts—physical and environmental, economic, social and cultural—on the life of the city.

Howard E. Mitchell

Part I

THEME: THE UNIVERSITY AND THE URBAN CRISIS

1. *Great Expectations*[1]

WARREN G. BENNIS

No one has expressed as well as William Butler Yeats the passion that underlies man's drive to know. Listen to the following lines:

> Civilization is looped together, brought
> Under a rule, under the semblance of peace
> By manifold illusion; but man's life is thought,
> And he, despite his terror, cannot cease
> Ravening through century after century,
> Ravening, raging, and uprooting that he may come
> Into the desolation of reality.

I chose those lines from Yeats to begin with tonight because there is a notion currently popular that this is a quiet time for universities. No time is quiet for universities. Universities are always in turmoil. No struggles are more anguished than those between ideas, between opposing views of the world, of reality, and such clashes occur every day on this campus, on every good campus in the country. If the universities are quiet, it is only the absence of sounds that were alien to the university spirit in the first place.

[1]Inaugural Address, University of Cincinnati, November 5, 1971.

I hope that our association at the University of Cincinnati will be a passionate, exhilarating, rewarding time, but not a quiet one.

In the weeks we have already spent together, you have learned something of my educational goals for our University of Cincinnati. And I have been learning too. The University community and the community-at-large have been extraordinarily kind and open with me. As a result, I have developed a set of high expectations: great expectations. Let me share those expectations with each of you: faculty, students, and directors, alumni, and friends, in turn.

THE STUDENT BODY

First, of the student body: I hope that you will continue to dramatize the primacy of learning as the central mission of the University. I hope that you will continue to see, with a clarity and sense of outrage that sometimes unnerves us who are not as young, those areas of the educational experience in need of reform. Until recently, I had always thought that Wordsworth's contention that the child is father of the man was an example of the Romantic fallacy. But in today's world of shifting values each generation has lessons to teach the last. It was students who exposed the multiversity for the unresponsive machine it had become. And it is the young who constantly remind us that bad education is more than another cause for concern, more than a reason to form expert task forces and compile reports. For the young, bad education is a crime. And they know. Because they are the victims. Do any of the spate of recent official reports on "the crisis in the classroom," however eloquent in their own right, make the outrage as poignantly felt as these six short lines by poet Richard Brautigan:

> I remember all those thousands of hours
> that I spent in grade school watching the clock,

waiting for recess or lunch or to go home.
Waiting: for anything but school
My teachers could easily have ridden with Jesse
James
for all the time they stole from me.

Brautigan served this time involuntarily. Happily, the University is not compulsory, but it too has intellectual wastelands. It is students upon whom we depend most for finding and exposing these. It is students who continue to be the very conscience of the University.

And I hope that you will scrutinize your own ideas and actions with as much vigor and candor as you have shown in your analysis of American institutions and society as a whole. The imagination that gave us, for want of another term, an exciting counter-culture was a young imagination—fresh, original. But good ideas have a way of attracting less imaginative imitators. Innovation becomes fashion. The counter-culture is as susceptible as any to this phenomenon. One has constantly to be on guard against faddism. I sometimes wonder if the campuses of the future are going to be covered with one geodesic dome after another, creating a landscape as dull as the bleakest cooky-cutter subdivision. I hope that the youth culture or counter-culture will continue to change, continue to find fresh areas to explore and will not settle simply for a different set of conventions, a new set of false gods.

Be critical, but remember that learning is self-activating. Don't wait to be turned on. No learning environment, even the most Utopian, can substitute for your own rage to know.

THE FACULTY

And second, of the faculty: Students are the raison d'etre of the university. Faculty are its very life. Today's faculty faces a unique challenge. There was a time when a teacher could regard himself as successful if he transmitted to his students some specialized truths, if he passed on to the next generation some limited body of knowledge. But in order to equip our students for an uncertain future, today's faculty must also teach their students how to learn. This forces us to look for new approaches to teaching, to find new settings for learning, even to rethink our definitions of the scholarly disciplines. More than any other body the faculty determine the values by which a university lives. When a university becomes known for its excellence and flexibility, it is because the faculty support and esteem excellence and flexibility.

Excellence in teaching largely determines the quality of learning in the University. But teaching transcends any narrow definition. Certainly, the faculty member whose classes overflow with enthusiastic, learning students is to be regarded as a good teacher. But the excellent researcher is also a good teacher. The teaching-scholarship conflict is an accepted one, but false. Who is to say that the individual who enlarges our knowledge of the world is less a teacher than the charismatic lecturer? Or that scholarly activity precludes teaching, as if the interaction of student and teacher, collaborating in the library, were not a learning situation? More often than not, the most productive scholars are the best teachers. After all, both activities require the same personal characteristics: mastery of one's field, intense motivation, personal discipline, and creativity. I hope that Cincinnati will take the lead in developing a broadened definition of what constitutes teaching and learning to replace the inadequate conventional notions.

I hope that you as faculty will demand more of the University as a learning environment. Many universities fail their faculty as learners. And some faculty shy away from the terror of a new idea and betray the very methods of inquiry. We all long for a climate of genuine conviviality, which is necessary to animate learning men and women.

The University of Cincinnati can become unique in its development of an atmosphere in which faculty as well as students are able to realize their highest intellectual aspirations. As the Faculty learn, so will the students.

In order to create a joyous and rewarding educational climate, we must begin to develop answers to the following questions: How do we develop an atmosphere in which faculty are able to satisfy their own needs for intellectual growth? How do we acknowledge continuous intellectual renewal? How do we encourage responsible experimentation without sacrificing competence and quality? And how do we develop a true collegiality and conviviality so that we can evaluate and learn from each other? Whether or not the faculty become learning men and women will depend on what answers to these basic educational questions can be found.

The university needs and values the expertise and the wisdom of its faculty. And it relies on the faculty to keep the spirit of academic freedom alive.

THE BOARD, ALUMNI, AND FRIENDS

Third, of the board of directors, the alumni, and friends of the University: I trust that the University of Cincinnati will continue to receive from its board the remarkable service and support it has known in the past. The board has a very special role in the life of the University. It brings to the campus a detachment and perspective, a sympathetic objectivity, that no other body in the University has. It facilitates all those activities that occur at the delicate membrane between campus and city, university and society. The directors have succeeded admirably in guiding the University, without ever losing sensitivity to the University's right to pursue its own goals according to its standards.

My hope of the board, the alumni, and the university's many friends in the community is only that you will expect more of us.

The University of Cincinnati has a commitment to this community that has been welded over more than a century and a half.

If I were seeking a new motto for our University I think I would choose one that Murray Seasongood, our distinguished professor of law, quoted when he was made professor emeritus at the age of eighty. Mr. Seasongood quoted what Michelangelo said at age eighty: "Ancora imparo—I am still learning."

I would choose that motto because it sums up what I hope, more than anything else, to achieve here, and that is to see this place become a center, not merely of youthful learning, but of lifelong learning.

There is no reason students must come only in four sizes, 18, 19, 20, and 21. There is good reason to believe that many might be better students if they spent two years doing something else. And there is ample reason to believe that there are thousands of people over thirty who would like to continue learning, and who could, with the proper opportunities, become committed and concerned scholars in our midst. I include among them the increasing number of men and women who find just one career not sufficiently satisfying or psychically rewarding, and in their forties or later wish to take up another.

I hope to see our University become the kind of seedbed where such seekers after knowledge can become, as I like to put it, "repotted"—putting forth healthy new roots in self-renewal.

I should like to see us call upon the wisdom and knowledge of a great many accomplished men and women who have never studied teaching, may not have any degrees at all, but who have proved by their lives and works that they have knowledge of infinite value to share, both with our students and faculty. I envision seminars where all of us can benefit from this experience.

CITY HALL AND THE UNIVERSITY: COMMAND POSTS FOR URBAN RENEWAL

A generation ago, Washington was the power center where young men could work the levers that had an impact on the world. Today, City Hall is where the action is, and the city itself is the focus of all the major problems that concern the young—crime, congestion, pollution, racism, alienation, drugs. Washington is furiously trying to find ways to funnel both money and power back to the cities. Yet our University has little more than vaguely advisory relationships to those, in City Council and elsewhere, who are wielding the levers of municipal power.

Properly, the University should be, along with City Hall, the command post of all the operations to reclaim, renew, rebuild, and revitalize the city. More of our student lawyers should be getting their day-to-day experience as helpers in legal aid and for consumer groups, our student architects working as interns on urban renewal, our learning sociologists accompanying case workers to the homes.

There are day-care centers that need starting and staffing, illiterates that need to be taught, addicts that need encounter therapy, neglected children who need a friendly voice and hand. The city around us is itself a university without walls.

A university serves a community and a state when it trains its professionals and educates its sons and daughters. But there are additional ways to serve. Cincinnati has never been a spectator city. It is a participant city, and the University shares this spirit. Our cooperative program with the city's fine police department exemplifies this commitment. Public safety is but one area of common concern that can benefit from the active cooperation of the University and the city.

Our goal can be no less than to provide continuous education. This will mean more adult education and greater emphasis on education at mid-career. It will mean devising new degree programs to meet changed needs. In the last analysis, it will mean a University of Cincinnati whose mission is no less than aiding each of us in his ceaseless quest to know.

And, finally, what should you expect of me, U. C.'s eighteenth president?

You should expect me to interpret the University to faculty, students, alumni, government, and community and seek to marshall their support for the proper interests of the University. You should expect me to see that our central administration is directed in a manner conducive to inquiry and education, and that it will be responsive and humane without wasting resources that might be otherwise used for educational purposes. You should expect me to be able to distinguish between the courage of wise convictions and blind stubbornness. You should expect me to help protect the University from complacency or mindlessness by insisting upon the very best appointments and by identifying new problems and opportunities. You should expect me to help create an educational climate of growth, of belief in the ceaseless quest to know, of openness and honesty, and to implement a truth-in-administration policy. You should expect me to bend every effort to defend the essential freedoms of the University and to make decisions that command understanding and respect, both within and without the University. And, most of all, you should expect me to embody in action all those virtues our universities and colleges have proved so capable of inspiring in others: an examined life, a spirit of inquiry and genuine experimentation, a life based on discovering new realities, of taking risks, suffering occasional defeat, and not fearing the surprise of the future.

In closing, I wonder how many of you sense the unique fortune U. C. enjoys in this city. So many universities now survive in a situation of debilitating hostility with the communities that surround them. Our relationship with the Community is one of affection and mutual respect, and from that we both reap enormous benefits. We have a great city; it needs us, we need it. There is much that is good about it, there is much in it that needs critical attention. Our students—and we are all students, really—should be considering what might be done about the things that are not right and should be learning from the things that are right.

I believe we would be wrong to consider these grounds and these buildings only as our University.

I suspect this is a time for tearing through walls, not building them, and I speak as much of walls of the mind as I do of walls of stone and ivy. I think this is a time for moving out of the rooms and fluorescent lights for the more penetrating light outside, and when that is impossible, for bringing that outside light in here for the illumination it can offer us. I think this is a time for preserving what we have that is good and for finding out what we need to make ourselves better.

I believe we can do this. But we must do it together: city and university, student and citizen, professor and student.

This University, this city, this time: they are ours. If we make the most of them, we will make this University the nation's greatest urban university—one like no other in the land.

I ask you to join me: let us tear down the walls between us all. . . . The night is gone; the light has come; a new day has begun.

Part II

FOCUS ON COMMUNITY: PHILADELPHIA

2. The Philadelphia Story

HOWARD E. MITCHELL

This is not the complete Philadelphia Story of university-community involvement. If space permitted, a more comprehensive report of the Philadelphia area would include activities at LaSalle, St. Joseph's, Beaver, and the Philadelphia College of Art as well as community colleges and other schools which ring the city. What was intended here was to obtain reports from the two largest institutions of higher learning in Philadelphia and one from a smaller college on the periphery of the metropolitan Philadelphia community which has established a program extending into the inner-city. The latter is represented by a paper written by President John R. Coleman and Paul E. Wehr of Haverford College. This relatively small, male, independent, but Quaker institution, founded in 1856, might be viewed as a model for programs that two other similar institutions in suburban Philadelphia—coeducational Swarthmore and female Bryn Mawr—might develop and compare their experience with.

It is also important in reading about the experiences of Philadelphia institutions of higher learning in societal processes and problems to be reminded of the history and impact of Quakers upon the life of the community both past and present. The Religious Society of Friends, called Quakers, built their first Meeting House in Philadelphia in

1693 on land given by William Penn. The early Friends were prominent in furthering the cause of religious and civil liberties. According to Howard H. Brinton (1958), they began to establish Quaker colleges in the first half of the nineteenth century. This followed the development of elementary and secondary schools, many of the first being in the Philadelphia area. From the very beginning, and at all levels of education, Quaker students were actively involved in the life of the surrounding community as an adjunct to their learning experience. When Coleman and Wehr report that one feature of the Educational Involvement Program at Haverford College included students actually living in the inner-city, this should come as no surprise to those who know of the long tradition of student Quaker work camps coordinated by the American Friends Service Committee at all levels of education.

Howard E. Mitchell's article begins the section on Philadelphia. He reflects on the experience gained in the first nine years of operating the Human Resources Center, University of Pennsylvania. He delineates the developing philosophy and some of the key issues and problems faced in operation of action-research and training programs in the context of service in the community. Then the papers by Cahill and Perry and by Lavell present detailed statements about two very different Human Resources Center programs, which do have two aspects in common. Both are concerned with extending the university's traditional leadership training function to include new populations: in one case, educationally privileged women in the suburbs and, in the other, leaders and potential leaders of disadvantaged communities. Both aim toward the development of unrealized human potential in order to organize communities or to change attitudes and institutions.

Herman Niebuhr's article concludes the section. He represents one of the early pioneers among university people involved in urban issues in the Philadelphia region. Like Duhl, Levine, Mitchell, and Lavell, Niebuhr was initially trained as a clinician; he migrated into a high administrative post at Temple University after getting his baptism as a director of programs between the university and the community. Both Niebuhr and Mitchell were introduced into the dynamics of community involvement as associate directors of the Ford Foundation-sponsored Philadelphia Council for Community Advancement (see Mitchell's article for reference to the scope and program of this experiment).

The socio-political climate of Philadelphia in the 1950's and the 1960's was one of political reform and a physical renaissance. Students of political science and urban design flocked to its institutions of higher learning to look more closely at these phenomena during the political regimes of Joseph S. Clark and Richardson Dilworth. It was in fact during this era that the first graduate department of city and regional planning was established in the Graduate School of Fine Arts at the University of Pennsylvania in 1951. Its initial staff was closely affiliated both in philosophy and functional ties with the newly formed and active City Planning Commission of Philadelphia under the leadership of Edmund Bacon. You will note in Mitchell's article about his experiences in developing the Human Resources Center, University of Pennsylvania, that it became affiliated with the Gradute Department of City and Regional Planning, after its first two years.

Finally, one of the central themes enunciated by Chermayeff and Tzonis (1971) has merit as one reviews these reports of university-community transactions on the Philadelphia scene.

> Mankind may learn quickly enough, for instance, that the availability of information through technological media alone is not enough to create human purpose and that direct, constant interaction between people, individually and in community, as well as concern for the well-being of all things in the environment is required. This is central to our theme

and why we emphasize the provision of the full gamut of human experience in the form of direct interaction between work, leisure and learning, between the private and the public realms and between the participating and the temporarily alienated. Identity is the complementary opposite to anonymity in the spectrum of community. Both these characteristic options in complementarity must be maximized to obtain full potential, thus inducing participation and involvement.

Similarly, these writers of the Philadelphia Story seem to be advocating how the contemporary university might become a part of a more balanced urban community, one in which both partners—university and the urban complex—gain from the development of mutually determined transactions. Others have suggested that this state of affairs will only be achieved if most universities first admit, like it or not, that they are thrust into the midst of the urban crisis and that the urban university in the slums certainly has interests different from the surrounding community. The Philadelphia group, however, points out areas of mutual interest largely consistent with the traditional, educational goals of the university and demonstrates how such educational programs might be engineered in such a manner as to aid in the solution of urban problems.

REFERENCES

Brinton, H. H. *Quaker education in theory and practice.* Pendle Hill Pamphlet, Number 9, Revised. Wallingford, Penna.: 1958.

Chermayeff, S., and Tzonis, A. *Shape of community: Realization of human potential.* Baltimore: Penguin Books, 1971.

3. The Human Resources Center of the University of Pennsylvania

HOWARD E. MITCHELL

Edward Potts Cheney, who wrote the definitive history of the University of Pennsylvania for the years 1740 to 1940 (Cheney, 1940),[1] interestingly begins with a chapter entitled, "The City." In this chapter he emphasizes the polarization of the Philadelphia community, between rich and poor, during pre-Revolutionary times. On the one hand, Cheney writes, "Philadelphia was, as has been observed, a rich city. It was possible by wholesale or retail trade to change a small business rapidly into a large one. A competence was easy, wealth not too difficult to obtain. There were already several well-established wealthy merchant families." Contrast this with his statements later in the same chapter, in which he writes, "There was much poverty in the city. The overseers of the poor were always busy; and we hear of widespread suffering and of special collections being made when there was an unusually hard winter. There was much disorder. . . . Crimes and misdemeanors were numerous and punishments were harsh.

[1]The distinguished historians, Dr. Roy Nichols, former Dean of the Graduate School of Arts and Sciences, The University of Pennsylvania, and his wife, Dr. Jeanette P. Nichols, have been engaged in writing an updated history of the University of Pennsylvania.

... Slaves were sent to the Court House at Second and Market Streets by their owners to be whipped for their misdemeanors." Into such a community Benjamin Franklin brought his belief in higher education, his energy, and his practical wisdom. These attributes gave birth to an institution. This paper relates some of the experiences of that institution, The University of Pennsylvania, approximately two hundred years later, in its response to the challenges of the urban environment.

Philadelphia today, as in Franklin's time, still struggles to understand and develop ways of bridging the gap between the affluent and the impoverished, the educated and the undereducated, the employed and the unemployed, the sheltered and the homeless. Current events make clear that unless we learn how to communicate across widening socio-economic class and racial group barriers, we can expect only violent dialogues to emit from the impoverished of the inner city and some affluent youth on our campuses.

The urban-based institution of higher learning, it is held here, is in a unique position to contribute a vitally needed new urban dialogue. J. Martin Klotsche, chancellor of the University of Wisconsin at Milwaukee, has effectively summarized arguments for why and how the urban university is or should be involved in urban problems in the book, *The Urban University and the Future of Our Cities* (Klotsche, 1966).

Throughout the nation today, Americans are looking to its schools and colleges—expectantly, urgently, as the principal agency for bringing about equality of opportunity and the fulfillment of the dream of democracy. Colleges and universities are occupied as never before with the complex problems of our metropolitan areas. In many ways this involves a rational approach to the persistent inequities of our urban society between the worlds of the "haves," "the have somes," and the "have nots." The urban university can provide a fresh point of view and devise new techniques of dealing with the unresolved problems of its disadvantaged neighbors, crime and poverty, and unequal educational and vocational opportunity as well as problems of housing, medical services, sanitation, transportation, and land use.

Reported here are reflections about a nine-year experience in establishing an illustrative university-based comprehensive community program. It is the story of a clinically-trained-turned-community-psychologist and his coworkers, and their efforts to bring some of the resources of a large urban-based university to bear on selected problems facing the city. Perspectives gained in the operation of the Human Resources Center,[2] University of Pennsylvania will be described.

It was the policy of the University of Pennsylvania under President Gaylord P. Harnwell to react with sensitivity to the important and pressing problems that related to the equality of opportunity for all citizens in their communal life. The best documentation of this is contained in President Harnwell's annual report for 1966 to the University alumni and friends. The report begins, "The American university is out of its ivory tower—if indeed it ever occupied one—and never before have its unique resources been so widely utilized for the general welfare of man and the quality of his environment as they are today [Harnwell, 1966]."

After outlining the involvement of University of Pennsylvania scholars in the affairs of man nationally and internationally, President Harnwell centered a large part of his report on the unique contributions of Pennsylvania as an urban university to its immediate environment. "The most serious problems of society are where the population is most dense, and a great urban university is uniquely suited to study them and contribute to their solutions. The city itself provides a laboratory. This is particularly true of

---

[2]As will be noted later, the Human Resources Center (HRC) was originally designated the Human Resources Program until its locus in the University changed in 1966.

an old, established city such as Philadelphia, with which the University of Pennyslvania has been intrinsically intertwined since its birth."

The experiences of the University to be shared with the reader here are those of the Human Resources Center, established in April, 1964 by the administration. The scope and thrust of the program are best understood if one looks briefly at two somewhat diverse lines of activity which provide, on the one hand, an historical background and, on the other hand, knowledge about the immediate stimulus for the Human Resources Center.

DEVELOPMENTAL FACTORS

Recognizing that the urban university must assist in reversing the tide of urban decline and actively participate in the redevelopment of its surrounding neighborhood, the University of Pennsylvania helped to create "University City." The West Philadelphia Corporation was established in 1959 by the University along with the Drexel Institute of Technology (later Drexel University), Philadelphia College of Pharmacy and Science, Presbyterian Hospital, and the Philadelphia College of Osteopathy, to revitalize the community in all of its central dimensions—education, recreation, housing, health, and other community services (Harnwell, 1971). Under the dynamic leadership of its Executive Vice President, Leo Molinaro, the West Philadelphia Corporation sparked imaginative programs and established itself as a sound medium of institutional-community interaction. The social engineering of the West Philadelphia Corporation has required great skill as it has had to work simultaneously hand-in-hand with city authorities, business, industry, the universities, and community groups in order to develop an outstanding center for scientific research. At the same time, it is involved in strengthening slum area schools and beautifying depressed neighborhoods, and its leadership has had to revitalize off-campus housing to the degree that University personnel will be attracted to live near the campus in University City. The latter activity serves to increase the potential for student-faculty relationships and to some degree reduce the impersonalization of the students' collegiate experience. Reference to the undergraduate student body points up the fact that action by a group of students in the winter of 1964 provided the immediate impetus for the establishment of the Human Resources Center.

Students at the University, like college students around the world, are attuned to the emergent values of society and are in the vanguard of freedom. Dating from the freedom rides, sit-ins, and other forms of direct action by Negro students joined by their white copatriots in the South in the mid-1950's, events have moved rapidly in respect to their involvement in social issues and political action. This new "Ferment on the Campus," as it has been called by David Mallery (1966), replaced the student apathy and disinterest noted by Professor Philip E. Jacob in the 1940's and early 1950's. Professor Jacob wrote the following about students of that era:

> A dominant characteristic of students in the current generation is that they are *gloriously contented* both in regard to their present day-to-day activity and their outlook for the future. Few of them are worried —about their health, their prospective careers, their family relations, the state of national or international society or the likelihood of their enjoying secure and happy lives. They are supremely confident that their destinies lie within their own control rather than in the grip of external circumstances (Jacob, 1957).

During the 1960's we witnessed as never before a degree of concern, sensitivity, and commitment by many young college students for society's problems. While the power structure of the community was deliberating courses of action, impetuous, courageous, dedicated youth demanded a response. Granted, these student expressions were often awkwardly expressed in an aggressively demanding style, but this behavior represented a desperate attempt by college youth to find ways to negotiate, from an extremely weak bargaining position, about affairs which concern them. It was in this climate that one student leadership group at the University presented President Harnwell with a nine-point action program concerning the hiring practices and apprenticeship policies of the building and construction trades engaged in raising new structures on the campus. In response to this inquiry, it was publicly announced that the University does have a responsibility—a genuine desire—to actively support equality of opportunity. With members of the student protest group in attendance, meetings were held with representatives of all building and construction contractors engaged in University work. President Harnwell made it eminently clear in these discussions that the University was committed to the democratic ideal and considered the antidiscrimination clause to be a vital part of every contract with them.

These discussions also made clear the opportunity for students, faculty, and administration to have a meaningful impact upon the life of people in the community, as well as an opportunity for students, faculty, and administration to widen their horizons and experience. The Human Resources Center was established as the administrative mechanism through which the resources of the University on all levels might be coordinated, in the areas of education and human and industrial relations, relating to social change and equal opportunity. A staff was organized responsible to the Office of the President, assisted in its policy-making by an Advisory Committee comprised of key faculty in education, the social sciences, law, social work, and in the labor and industry departments of the University. Jefferson B. Fordham, then Dean of the Law School, headed the committee.

The initial phase of the Human Resources Center covered the period from April, 1964 to the end of June, 1966. The projects carried out during the first two years were viewed as pilot programs or laboratories in which the University, in the context of service to the community, was able to fuse research, development, and training.

THE UNI-DIRECTIONAL PHASE, 1964-1966

This period can be called the Uni-Directional Phase because most of the programs developed and implemented were not planned to have a major effect upon changing the University in attitude, operation, or structure.[3] Primary concern was directed toward how best to bring the resources of the University to bear on some problem external to its physical self. Implicit was the notion "that the University must help those poor deprived people out there." For the most part the issues considered were those brought to the door of the Office of the President by community groups, as well as local and national leaders, who requested advice and assistance in the solution of urban problems. Many of these problems were those the administration felt the leadership of the Greenfield Center for Human Relations and/or the Graduate School of Education might have interest in. Since the leadership of these units had other priorities, the Human Resources Center was established. Besides, it was not fashionable in most parts of the University to engage in action-research in a service context. It was felt that by initially operating out of the Office of the President, assisted by counsel from the Advisory Committee, the program might more effectively offer interested faculty and stu-

[3]The Appendix contains a complete listing of HRC projects and the academic offerings which have been developed from the action-research from 1964 to 1973 divided into two time periods.

dents the opportunity to become engaged in this new laboratory.

The author was invited to return to the University from leave, where he had been serving as Associate Director of the Philadelphia Council for Community Advancement (PCCA). This latter organization was the fifth urban experiment then being conducted by the Ford Foundation to see if an "umbrella-type" structure could do something about the problems of the blighted areas of large urban communities. "These organizational structures," it has been stated elsewhere, "were the prototypes of the community-action groups in large urban areas under the war-on-poverty programs. The PCCA, like many other community-action organizations in the current poverty campaign, was literally pulled apart by external and internal power struggles [Mitchell, 1970]."[4] Marris and Rein (1967) give an excellent objective account of the PCCA experience in their book *Dilemmas of Social Reform.*

Therefore, the author entered into the leadership role of the Human Resources Program in 1964 hopeful that the University was committed, in a more coordinated manner, to use its new mechanism to bring some of its expertise and resources to bear on critical urban problems. The University of Pennsylvania, like other urban-based universities, had long demonstrated involvement and commitment to the urban situation. Closely related to the physical and political renaissance of Philadelphia in the 1950's emerged an academic leadership which developed the Department of City and Regional Planning as the first graduate teaching program in this vital area. More importantly for our purposes here, President Harnwell's administration from 1953 to 1970 was not only a significant period in the physical growth of the University,

---

[4]One of the two most significant indigenous-led community development programs begun in the 1960's in the U.S. was negotiated with and received a large part of its initial funding from the Ford Foundation via PCCA. We refer here to the Opportunities Industrialization Center.

but the period in which this urban university moved toward the development of an institutional arrangement which would provide a more effective relationship between the University and its neighbors. We refer here to the aforementioned West Philadelphia Corporation under Leo Molinaro's direction. His leadership assisted in laying the groundwork for some of the first Human Resources Program's projects. He was extremely perceptive not only of the dynamics of the surrounding community, but of the politics and operation of the University and his broker role between the two. The value and skill of such a person were soon revealed by his knowledge of how to intervene into different worlds and effect planned change.[5] Increasingly we understood that to most populations with whom we would be dealing, the University symbolized the "have world" and successful delivery of an action-research or training program depended upon how skillful one became in intervening into different subsystems of the community.

INTERVENTION TO EFFECT PLANNED CHANGE

The author had thought a great deal about the problem of service delivery and intervention strategies as a member of a clinical team extending psychotherapy to entire family groups in the home setting (Friedman, *et al.,* 1965). From this experience a bias crystallized toward viewing such problems in social system terms. Occupying a central place in the operational philosophy of HRP was the concept of intervention strategies based upon the importance of mutual determination of goals by the change agent (therapist or university) and the designated client system (patient or "have-not" community or population).

[5]Planned change is defined here as a rational process in which we attempt to bring scientific knowledge to bear on social problems in which there is mutual goal-setting by one or both parties and as nearly as possible an equal power-ratio (Bennis, 1966).

With the increasing polarization between rich and poor, black and white, urbanite and suburbanite, faculty and student, administration and student, the HRP staff soon developed interest in seeking to understand how one might effectively intervene into unfamiliar worlds in order to bring about planned change. This research interest is basic to all the action programs developed, whether in the low-income minority area of Mantua adjacent to the campus, in Arkansas, or within the campus community.

From the author's clinical experience he recalls the challenge and rebuff from patients diagnosed as schizophrenic or alcoholic as he sought to enter their world as an agent of change and to assist them in bringing about the behavioral and attitudinal alterations they sought. It was recognized that new clients had often waited outside any helping system and had understandably developed a defensiveness and suspiciousness toward any member of the establishment. Often an alcoholic would ask "the intervener" if he had suffered from his illness. When the answer would be in the negative, the implication—often stated directly and with strong invective—was that if the helping agent had not shared the anguish and debilitating effects of his illness, he could never be fully sensitive, empathic, and helpful to him.

In such instances it was the author's approach to appreciate fully the client's feelings and why at best he might be ambivalent toward others intervening into his life. We soon faced much the same situation in our action programs as we sought to bring the resources of the University to bear on human problems manifest in blighted urban communities. We were initially viewed as part of the outside establishment which is often perceived as intervening only to further personal or institutional self-interest. With the heightened racial feelings in our society, many blacks and whites are no longer seeking ways of communicating across cultural barriers. Aaron Wildavsky, writing in the journal *Public Interest* (Wildavsky, 1968), states that many white liberals have developed an "empty-headed blues." He says, "they feel bad. They know the sky is about to fall in. But they can't think of anything to do. Having been too sanguine and too self-righteous about their own part in the civil rights movement, they are too easily prey to despair when their contribution is rejected by those they presumed to help." Every day we witness blacks and whites withdrawing to their separate camps, on the one hand to examine their white racism, on the other to find their black identities. Both seem to forget or to ignore the fact that technological advances in communication and greater mobility have already committed culturally diverse communities to increased transactions. With so many liberal individuals and agencies torn between a nagging guilt and a secret desire to turn their back on demanding clients, our experience has in many ways been a refreshing contrast. This was not achieved, however, until we began to realize the serious limits of our expertise and how in many ways we needed the client system as much as they needed the resources of the University.

About this time this clinical perspective was influenced by reading a dialogue between the authors Ralph Ellison and Robert Penn Warren in the latter's book, *Who Speaks for the Negro* (Warren, 1965). Although the dialogue centers upon defining who are "culturally deprived" individuals, it has institutional implications as well. The exchange between the authors is as follows:

> *Ellison:* It's like this notion of the culturally deprived child—one of those phrases which I don't like—as I have taught white middle-class young people who are what I call "culturally deprived." They are culturally deprived because they are not oriented within the society in such a way that they are prepared to deal with its problems.

> *Warren:* It's a different kind of cultural deprivation, isn't it? And actually a more radical one.

Ellison: That's right, but they don't even realize it. These people can be much more troubled than the child who lives in the slum and knows how to exist in the slum.

Warren: It's more mysterious, what's happening to him—the middle-class child?

Ellison: Yes, it's quite mysterious, because he has everything, all of the opportunities, but he can make nothing of the society or of his obligations. And often he has no clear idea of his own goals.

THE BI-DIRECTIONAL PHASE, 1966–1973

From our initial engagement with community groups we began to think seriously about not only intervention strategies but the mutual benefit gained in collaborative relationships outside the campus. Both formal and informal discussion in and out of the Advisory Committee took place.

Emerging from these discussions was the realization that if action-research was to be carried out for the mutual benefit of community and university, the HRP needed to be given an academic home. Internal negotiations began, resulting in the decision in April, 1966 to bring the Human Resources Program into the Institute for Environmental Studies, which until 1972 was the interdisciplinary research unit of the Graduate School of Fine Arts. Simultaneously, the administration announced the appointment of the Director of the Human Resources Program, as the university's first Professor of Human Resources, in the Department of City and Regional Planning of the Graduate School of Fine Arts. Little did we know that at that time a significant number of students in the Graduate School of Fine Arts—especially prospective planners, architects, landscape architects, and urban designers—were clamoring for new educational inputs. The notion of advocacy planning had been intellectually pioneered by two young faculty members (Davidoff and Reiner, 1962; Davidoff, 1965) and the students wanted the opportunity to engage in field work as advocate planners for indigenous community groups as a fully accredited part of their professional education.

This new institutional arrangement for HRP made it possible to develop an operational philosophy which clearly enunciated that programs were engaged in for the mutual benefit of community and university. Associated with the above has been, however, the continued problem of interpreting the role of the Center in the University community. One wishes in this respect that more people had read and had been influenced by Nevitt Sanford's article showing the past respectability of action research (Sanford, 1970). Our problem with our University colleagues was in first distinguishing our role in action-research from that of being engaged in action *per se.*

Although not always recognized by University colleagues, the activities of HRP from the beginning were viewed with sensitivity not only to its role in university-community relations, but consistent with the University's basic function of research and teaching. With the new academic alignment, program was based upon activities which have implications for teaching in the Graduate School of Fine Arts and research which will enhance knowledge about intervention strategies to effect better public and private service for a wider range of citizens. The laboratory of choice for such study is the larger community and often in a service context. This does not mean that the HRP, as part of the University, was ever interested in rendering service *per se* to community groups.

We took a cue largely from both undergraduate and graduate students in community psychology, law, social work, education, medicine, and urban planning—who ask that part of their education include a clinical experience directly in the context of the processes of social change. Moreover, this is not new when aspects of medical training are considered. Teaching hospitals maintain clinics as an essential aspect of such training. These "community service" clinics provide the teaching material essential to the student. Some may argue that teaching hospitals maintain clinics out of their altruism toward the indigent and suffering poor. Although such a view is often valuable in public relations, clinics are established and maintained because an array of patients are required as teaching material. Happily the community benefits as well.

Every request for program funding of HRP projects has included a bibliographic review of the literature in order to develop and enunciate a conceptual framework, as well as provision for project evaluation as funds, knowledge, and personnel permit. We have always characterized the Center's programs as action-research. Action programs are not the business of the University. It is our conviction that we have not fully utilized for scholarship and teaching purposes community-based laboratories. The most meaningful of these laboratories are often those developed in collaboration with consumer groups of public and private services in the community. They provide a strategic opportunity to develop and redirect theoretical and empirical inquiries into the community in the context of the dynamics of community processes.

Further growth became possible in 1968 when a gift from the 1907 Foundation was designated for the endowment of a chair in Urbanism and Human Resources, and the author was named its first incumbent. In addition, it was at this time that the Human Resources Program was enlarged into a Center, which included a planning and research and a field-service division. Although these developments did much to reaffirm the belief that traditional walls were being broken down, both within the university and between the university and the surrounding community, funds were not budgeted to man these divisions. The Center, like other new university programs, suffered because no university, to the author's knowledge, ever looks at its total priorities. New programs are always thought of in terms of new funding and few universities have allocated sizable support for the growing number of urban research centers.

For example, in the Foreword of The Urban Institute's directory of such centers it is stated, "The growth of urban research centers in the universities across the nation has been phenomenal. Such centers in the early 1960's numbered only about two dozen. In 1967, there were about 80. Today we identify close to 200. Other universities also carry out some urban research in what they might designate as 'centers.' This growth represents a problem-solving potential of considerable magnitude [Urban Institute, 1969]." Yet, if one examines the Institute's directory, one notes how little financial support is budgeted by most universities for this activity. It is interesting to speculate that many centers were established with the university under duress, as was our case and that of The Urban Center at Columbia. How many have been developed as integral missing links to knowledge in the university's educational storehouse? Trying to sell to colleagues and administration that these laboratories are important and should be utilized consistent with the basic purposes of the university has required continuous effort. At the same time the Center has sought to interpret the difference between the intent of its efforts and a growing number of off- and on-campus community projects engaged in by other faculty and administrative personnel. The HRC staff has held that urban problems approached in a community laboratory should be taken as seriously as more traditional educational issues on campus. The nature of the urban condition is such that it requires the highest level of scholarship. Yet, it is appalling how many university faculty engage in a community-based project without even stopping to review what is known about the new population with whom they are to have contact or stopping to consult with colleagues similarly engaged.

These observations as well as others were documented in the sumer of 1969 by an evaluation carried out by HRC staff of sixteen University of Pennsylvania community-related projects. The research methodology consisted of reviewing project planning in terms of design, project implementation, and documentation via interviewing the principal investigator. We learned such programs were primarily for high school students residing in the University City area. Funding agencies for such activities included Federal, state, and local authorities, the Philadelphia Board of Education, civic groups, and private foundations. Although a majority of the projects received some funds from the University of Pennsylvania, most project directors were seeking supplemental grants at the time of the study. The survey indicated that faculty members frequently initiated projects and were usually provided with insufficient financial assistance to plan adequately and design forthcoming programs.

The study also pointed out that faculty and student involvement were limited in three key areas: the number of participating faculty and students, the time spent in actual faculty and community contact, and the number of people reached by university-related projects. Although participating faculty freely volunteered their time and expertise to community programs, most projects provided no financial compensation to community participants and involved only a small sector of the adjacent University City population. Fifty percent of the projects involved less than 30 community residents.

In the final stages of program evaluation and analysis, it was revealed that a majority of the projects did not have an explicit statement of the scope or effectiveness of the program. Many of the projects had only semidocumentation, while twenty-five percent had planned no documentation.

The interview data also revealed that many faculty so engaged needed to view their project independently from any other such activity associated with this or another campus. For example, it was as if it was important for a given man that his project be viewed as the first tutorial project for minority youth in order for it to be of intrinsic importance. This view was held by faculty who would discredit those in their field who failed to show the relation of knowledge about a contemporary phenomenon to previous research and discovery.

EXTERNAL-INTERNAL PROGRAM LINKS

In light of the above discussion as well as the bi-directional operational philosophy of HRC, we felt it important to understand in the context of the social systems of the university and the community how programs develop, the feedback of learning from the collaborative relationship with the community, and the resulting impact upon other components in the university system. Because of space limitations, these external-internal functional linkages will be illustrated only by a leadership training program, jointly planned with an indigenous community organization in late 1967. The linkages are indicated in Figure 1.

Like the establishment of the HRC, the initial impetus for this development grew out of a concern articulated by students. A poverty seminar was conducted by the author with eight graduate planning students in the spring semester, 1967. Toward the middle of the seminar the students petitioned the Department of City and Regional Planning to permit them to serve their required summer internship as advocate planners in the Mantua area of West Philadelphia. It was reasoned that it would be profitable if all eight made available their developing professional skills to the Young Great Society, Incorporated (YGS), an indigenously-led community development organization operating in a predominantly black area.

While contact was being made to present our tentative plans to the YGS two white professionals in Mantua asked

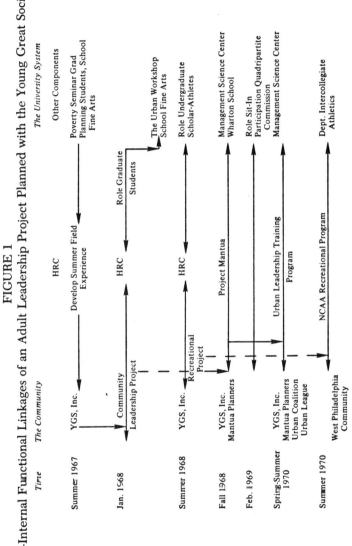

FIGURE 1

External-Internal Functional Linkages of an Adult Leadership Project Planned with the Young Great Society, Inc.

to meet with the author and his students. We agreed to meet with them to express the intent of the intervention into Mantua, and we were forcefully told not only would we be unwelcome but that it would be dangerous for the two white female students to be in the area and besides they had knowledge that the real intent of our intervention "is to sell the facts you collect to the City Planning Commission for $5,000."[6]

Attempts to meet with the leadership of the YGS were delayed and finally the community group rejected the invitation of planning students to work with them. The alleged basis of the rejection was that the students and the Center had developed the program before consulting YGS. Reference in this respect was to an informal communication to a local foundation asking whether a proposal to cover expenses incurred in the summer training project might be submitted if the YGS agreed to cooperate.

Three months following the YGS rejection, the author was surprised to receive a telephone call from Mr. Herman Wrice, President of YGS, stating "Doc, we need to get together and plan a training program with you at the University because we don't have enough manpower for our programs." Under joint sponsorship with YGS, the Adult Leadership Training Program became a reality early in 1968 through funds under Title I of the Higher Education Act matched by the University. This is illustrative of the kind of collaborative relationship we began to develop with neighbors off-campus in which goals and program implementation were mutually determined.[7]

A "training of trainers" technique was adopted which we have utilized in other action-research projects. Six

[6]The tape of this confrontation with the two white protectors of the black Mantua community has been useful as a training aid in helping students and other trainees to understand the dynamics of community development and the key role played by significant parties.

[7]We consciously attempted to define operationally and test Warren Bennis' concept of a collaborative relationship (Bennis, 1967).

YGS leaders were the trainers and each led a problem-solving seminar three nights a week for six weeks on the University campus under the supervision of the HRC staff. Another series of seminars on the same schedule followed. The seminars provided free and open discussion of social problems in such areas as education, housing, recreation, urban renewal, neighborhood development, and city planning. Six graduate students, four from city planning and one each from psychology and social work, functioned as liaisons between the YGS seminar leaders and the HRC staff. They had the responsibility of feeding each seminar group factual information and other resource materials and personnel.

Over 160 persons, half of them men, participated. The large majority were 18-20 years of age and residents of West Philadelphia. They responded with enthusiasm to the democratic learning atmosphere and controversial subject matter. One of the outcomes was the suggestion that YGS and HRC provide a summer recreational program for low-income, largely minority youngsters living near the campus.

It was reasoned that this program might be planned in such a manner as to promote the human potential of both the participating youngsters and the university scholar-athletes who would serve as operating personnel. Two of the student-athletes were brought into the planning process with the YGS leadership and were given the job of not only formulating the research proposal but presenting it to The Philadelphia Foundation for funding. Later these undergraduates reported that the preparation and successful negotiation of the proposal before the Foundation was the most difficult and important learning experience throughout the project.

From these initial contacts with the University both Mr. Herman Wrice, of the YGS, and Mr. Andrew Jenkins, of the Mantua Community Planners, quickly learned how to make strategic use of sources of power and influence within the University. Working with Professor Russell L.

Ackoff, of the University's Management Science Center, Project Mantua was begun in the fall of 1968. The thrust of this program was that, once the Mantua community leadership determined what it needed in the way of advice, technical assistance, or contact with governmental policy-makers and planners, the participating University personnel would attempt to provide them. This led to Wrice's key role in the student-led sit-in of the main administration building on campus in February, 1969, and his later serving as a member of the Quadripartite Commission.[8]

As shown in Figure 1, the Urban Leadership Training Program derived directly from Project Mantua. Twenty-two former gang leaders were recruited to participate in a twenty-one week program devoted to directing their energies toward more constructive goals.

There is an indirect linkage between the initial YGS-HRC Recreational Project in 1968 and the NCAA Recreational Program started in the summer of 1970. It was necessary in the conduct of the YGS-HRC 1968 Recreational Project to seek and obtain the cooperation of the Department of Intercollegiate Athletics for use of University recreational facilities. Mr. Fred Shabel, Director of the above unit, showed great insight into how his department might change and give greater emphasis to a community recreational program which now is an integral part of his total program.

An even more complete chronology of programming for minority community youth on campus than is presented in Figure 1 might well begin with the initial HRC project. This project was a six-week residential, educa-

[8]The Quadripartite Commission on University-Community Development was established by the Board of Trustees as a result of the six-day student sit-in protesting the research policy of the University City Science Center and demanding that land and low-income housing be provided for West Philadelphia residents displaced by the Science Center. Its membership included trustees, faculty, students, and community representatives.

tional, and vocational program for 100 Philadelphia area youth, Negro and white, who were undereducated and unemployed. Sixty-seven of the participants were or had been active urban gang members. To the best of the author's knowledge this marked the first formal use of all University facilities by such a population. The lasting generalization from that project in this respect is that when young citizens who have been forced to live second class are given a first class environment they mainly respond first class.

Dents in the HRC Ego

Finally, as one reflects on this nine-year experience one is aware of dents made in the collective HRC ego and idealism. We had hoped that the University would respond to the urban crisis in a more coordinated manner and that HRC would have proven itself to have a management capability which would have enabled it to play an integral role in this development. Such a role, we saw with increasing clarity, is consistent with the basic purpose of the University. We have come to realize however, that the power and politics of academia are not so different from those in the larger community. There has been a bandwagon effect operating within universities in regard to urban and minority affairs. Many skilled in grantsmanship have quickly climbed aboard and since no university to our knowledge has comprehensively planned and modeled its approach to the community, it responds mainly following a crisis. On these occasions the university is most happy to have any of its administration and/or faculty willing to do anything about "those problems." We maintain that under these circumstances, the same degree of scholarship that administration and faculty require in their own disciplines and traditional pursuits is not often demonstrated. And anyone with clinical experience knows that community clients, like emotionally deprived clients, soon know whether the so-called helping agent or professional has entered into a relationship primarily for his own vested interests and needs or for those of the client.

On the other hand, a perspective gained in reflecting on encounters with the community is the importance of remaining hopeful about the prospect of social and institutional change. The loss of idealism in this respect, which means becoming cynical when in contact with groups long denied opportunity and the rewards of power in our society, is defeating. The best ego support[9] of this attitude derives from those instances in which HRC staff are able to discern that their efforts have effected a small ripple in the large pond of institutional change of the University. Perhaps the best illustration of this was the responsiveness of the University administration to the recommendations forthcoming from the project entitled, "Minority Employment in the Construction Trades."

Using the University of Pennsylvania's ninety million dollars of campus construction as the principal laboratory, this program sought to: (1) conduct research into the building industry, current government programs, and groups working in this area; (2) coordinate employment and training programs with community groups; and (3) develop a model plan for increasing utilization of nonwhites in employment in the University of Pennsylvania's building program. The research was published in the form of a technical report to the administration of the University.[10] The University responded by establishing functional groups to examine the recommendations and suggest action. From these discussions the HRC project

[9]Other sources of ego support came from the always available and wise counsel of such Advisory Committee members as its chairman, Jefferson B. Fordham, Dean of the Law School; George W. Taylor, Harnwell Professor of Industry; and Everett Lee, Professor of Sociology.
[10]Copies of this study (Human Resources Center, 1969) were disseminated to other universities, institutions, and building agencies after it was rendered to the administration.

team was asked to continue to monitor efforts to implement equal employment by participation in a University of Pennsylvania Task Force on Employment of Minority Workers and in the President's Committee on Equal Opportunity.

At the time of writing the HRC staff approached 1973, reevaluating its role under a new administration. Basic to this role reevaluation the staff raised questions which might be raised by most operatives in university-based urban centers since the majority receive little or no university funding: In what further ways may the efforts of the Center be directed to provide uniquely a laboratory for faculty and students to bring their interest and scholarship to bear on critical urban problems? What might be done to attract greater commitment from the university for such environmentally-based learning laboratories? These questions seem equally important to those concerned with the development and future of community psychology. Moreover, it is important that universities take time to conceptualize the nature of their relationships to the urban scene and plan their involvement more systematically.

APPENDIX

UNI-DIRECTIONAL PHASE: 1964–1966

Projects

Arkansas Project: Feasibility Study. Undertaken by the Human Resources Center at the request of the Jane and John Martin Foundation to study the potential and problems of an interracial residential center for disadvantaged children at a chosen site in Southwest Arkansas.

Community Involvement Council. Technical and consultative services were provided to this student-led organization which coordinated information on a wide range of volunteer activities in which some 800 undergraduates annually participate.

Counselor Institute and Follow-Up Workshops. A three-week summer institute with follow-up workshops, to increase the professional competence of city high school guidance counselors in their work with students from low-income and minority groups.

Residential, Educational, and Vocational Program. A six-week residential, educational, and vocational program on the campus for 100 unemployed Philadelphia youth, Negro and white. This served as a pilot project for the Job Corps training centers now operating across the country under the Economic Opportunity Act of 1964.

Literacy Project. The Human Resources Center designed the evaluation for a literacy training program run by the Philadelphia School District and the Department of Welfare, Commonwealth of Pennsylvania for adult illiterates. The evaluation included comparisons of 1) results obtained by certified and noncertified teachers and 2) results under two different learning systems employed in the project.

Philadelphia Schools Study. A study of the impact of racial isolation upon educational performance in the Philadelphia schools, completed at the request of the United States Civil Rights Commission. The results of the study were included in the Commission's publication, *Racial Isolation in the Public Schools.*

Project College Bound. A six-week summer program for Philadelphia high school graduates from low-income backgrounds who had been accepted at colleges, but had specific educational deficiencies.

School Administrators' Seminar Evaluation. A self-evaluative design for the Philadelphia School District's seminar series on Integrated Quality Education. Provision for feedback enabled participants to perceive attitude changes and common problems and conflicts.

Courses

Education in Large Urban Areas. To prepare teachers for the challenge of the inner-city school, this course was taught in the University's graduate teacher-intern program. The course focused on factors affecting education in major cities with special attention to the culturally disadvantaged child.

Negro History and Culture. A 13-week televised course carried by two local stations was sponsored by the Human Resources Program. The course, covering historical, social, and cultural factors contributing to the suppression of the American Negro and responses to the suppression, was offered for credit in the University's College of General Studies.

Urban Crisis and the Schools. A televised course for which credit could be obtained from the College of General Studies pertaining to the changing urban community, social problems precipitated by urbanization, and their effect on education.

BI-DIRECTIONAL PHASE: 1966–1973

Projects

The Adult Leadership Training Program in Home and Neighborhood Self-Help Projects. Administrated in conjunction with the Young Great Society, with the goal of training indigenous youth and adults residing in an economically depressed area near the University in skills directly related to community improvement, action, and leadership. Over 160 persons participated.

Arkansas Planning Project: The Johnny Cake Child Study Center. The Human Resources Center played a key role in the planning and development of this institution in Mansfield, Arkansas. The long-range planning goal is to determine how children growing up in a rural institution can move with minimal difficulty into the larger urban community.

Career Development Institute. A three-week summer institute to promote, among counselors and teachers working with noncollege-bound youth, greater understanding of the nature of diverse career opportunities.

Community Hospital Affirmative Action Program. Three private, nonprofit, short-term community hospitals located just west of the city of Philadelphia sought advice from HRC in meeting the demands of civil rights groups who felt the institutions had been discriminatory in the hiring and promotion of minority workers. The Center was engaged to study the allegations and to devise an affirmative action program which would best meet the demands of the community group while serving hospital needs.

The Community Leadership Seminar. A series of ten training sessions for a group of indigenous community leaders. Planning with the leaders resulted in a program emphasizing fund procurement and management, goal definition and attainment, and increasing awareness of the various governmental systems which affect community organizations' development and functioning.

Evaluation of City Summer Recreation Programs. A study undertaken on subcontract for the United States Department of Labor of all Philadelphia recreational programs staffed under grants from that Department.

Evaluation of Job Loan and Urban Venture Corporation. A study of the functioning of this nonprofit corporation created by eight Philadelphia banks for the purpose of lending money to minority entrepreneurs unable to obtain funds through normal channels.

Evaluation of University-Community Projects. A study of the scope and characteristics of sixteen University-based projects. Most of the projects served high school students residing in the University area.

Exploratory Study of Economically Marginal Students. An investigation of differences in experiences of socioeconomically marginal versus nonmarginal University students in order to plan more effectively their educational experience.

Grass Roots Design. A housing study developed by two graduate students in the Department of Architecture, which the Human Resources Center helped to finance and direct. The primary aim was to determine the kinds of low-cost housing designs best suited to the needs of their inhabitants.

Lincoln-Darby Project.   In a cooperative venture with Lincoln University and a settlement house in Darby, Pennsylvania, the Human Resources Center helped design and implement an analysis of Darby to provide a substantial pool of knowledge about housing, social services, and community services. In addition to providing facts for planning and activating change in the community studied, the contacts between the participating institutions and their individual participants were enlarged.

Mini-School Evaluation.   In conjunction with the planning for the Mantua-Powelton Mini-School, the Human Resources Center designed an evaluative plan to help measure the effectiveness of a unique community-based school program.

Minority Employment Project.   This project has undergone two phases. The first, resulting in *A Report to President Gaylord P. Harnwell on University of Pennsylvania Employment in the Construction Trades,* was an investigation of the use of minority trainees, supervisors, and contractors on University construction sites. The second phase has been the establishment of a consortium of Philadelphia universities and urban institutions, in cooperation with unions and contractors, dedicated to planning for the utilization of nonwhites on the construction sites associated with the participating institutions.

New Town Study Inputs.   Beckett New Town is a proposed new community of 6,300 acres in Gloucester County, New Jersey, approximately 15 miles south of Central Philadelphia. The project will contain a diverse and balanced program of housing, supported by a full range of commercial uses, schools and community facilities, open space and parks, light industrial development, and the necessary supporting utilities and roadways. The Center was engaged to do the social planning, demographic studies, leisure time, recreational, and job training inputs for the proposed Beckett New Town.

Penn-Morgan State Project. Operating out of Human Resources Center offices, this project enabled various departments and faculty at the University of Pennsylvania to enter into a collaborative relationship with counterparts at Morgan State College in Baltimore. This involved faculty and student exchanges and joint research projects especially with regard to problems of the inner city in education and social work.

Pestalozzi International Children's Village Project. A research design was developed and its implementation supervised by the director of the Center, to measure interaction between nationality groups in the Village itself and also the interaction between the Village and its neighboring town of Trogen, Switzerland.

Philadelphia Demographic Study. The demography project is assembling and analyzing census and other data that can provide to community organizations a better basis for planning for their community's welfare than has hitherto been available. Data of interest include items on income, education, unemployment, family composition, age and sex distribution, morbidity and mortality rates, housing, and mobility. Certain trends will be noted and some projections made.

Police-Community Conflict in the Urban Community. This theme has been of continuing interest and has led to several studies including: The Philadelphia Police between 1840–1860 as an example of establishment of a *modern* police force; a study of law enforcement in early Boston, dealing primarily with the problem of maintaining social order in a preindustrial society; and a study of Britain s᾽ new unit-beat system specifically designed for community involvement and increased efficiency.

Project Exploration and Discovery. Conducted with 38 tenth grade students from the Philadelphia public schools, with emphasis on preparation for and strengthening of liberal arts, cultural curriculum. The College of General Studies is now conducting this program.

Recreation Workshop. A six-week program of planned athletic, recreational, and cultural activities for children between the ages of nine and fourteen from a low-income minority area. Conducted for two summers, it served 96 and 75 children respectively, using scholar-athletes as counselors.

Suburban Training Program (STP). Two year-long programs of weekly sessions to acquaint suburban women with the problems of urban ghettos so that they can interpret these problems to their own communities and become encouragers of creative and constructive social change.

Suburban Education Program. An outgrowth of the Suburban Training Program composed of geographical clusters of STP graduates and interested others. The clusters maintain contact with the Human Resources Center as a resource while autonomously conducting educational or action projects according to the group's interest.

Suburban Potential. A "correspondence course" following the goals and direction of the Suburban Training Program for suburban women residing out of the Philadelphia area. In addition to receiving reading, participants respond with questions, comments, and suggestions.

Summer Intern Program in Urban Affairs. Conducted for six years for the managerial staff of United Parcel Service. Through the medium of seminars, reading, field trips, and a live-in experience at Henry Street Settlement House in New York City, the program is designed to help both individual managers and the company as a whole realize responsibilities and constructive action which must be considered by urban institutions.

Survey for University Council on Urbanism. Assistance to the Council in conducting a survey of the University's nineteen schools and research centers, in developing interdisciplinary faculty seminars on urban problems, and in related efforts to chart a university-wide approach to the study of urban life.

United Parcel Service Evaluation. A study of the Summer Intern Programs run for United Parcel Service middle-managers at the Human Resources Center, Henry Street Settlement House in New York City, and the Better Boys Foundation in Chicago.

Courses

Special Readings Seminar. Independent research seminar for graduate students in City Planning. Each student investigated one aspect of American urban poverty.

Urban Crisis and the Church. Taught for the Episcopal Seminary emphasizing the changing urban community, the problems and resources available, and the positive role the clergy and church can play in urban change.

Urban Educational Planning. A City Planning course dealing with urban educational planning within the context of city and human resource development.

Urban Social Change. A course in the Graduate School of Fine Arts emphasizing the use of social system models, the vast number of issues affecting planned change and the application of models to a variety of urban systems and situations.

The Urban Workshop. Established in response to the expressed needs of the community around the University of Pennsylvania and to provide an opportunity for students in planning and architecture programs to exercise their acquired skills and training in such a way as to benefit both the students and the community.

Seminar on Women as Agents of Social Change. Growing out of three years' experience in the Suburban Training Program, a seminar was offered in Spring 1973 in the College of Thematic Studies, under auspices of Penn Women's Studies Planners. The seminar was planned to acquaint undergraduates first with the contributions of women to social reform in the 19th and early 20th centuries, and then with the efforts of women in the Philadelphia region who are attempting to bring about social change as a solution for present-day problems. Their activities were examined in the context of opportunity for self-realization in the combined role of homemaker and change agent.

REFERENCES

Bennis, W., Benne, K., & Chin, R. *The planning of change.* New York: Holt, Rinehart & Winston, 1966.

Cheyney, E. P. *History of the University of Pennsylvania 1740–1940.* Philadelphia: University of Pennsylvania Press, 1940.

Davidoff, P. Advocacy and pluralism in planning. *Journal of the American Institute of Planners,* 1965, XXXI, 331–338.

Davidoff, P., & Reimer, T. A choice theory of planning. *Journal of the American Institute of Planners,* 1962, XXVIII, 103–115.

Friedman, A., *et al. Psychotherapy for the whole family.* New York: Springer Publishing Co., 1965.

Harnwell, G. P. An environment for learning. *Proceedings of the American Philosophical Society,* 1971, 115, 170–186.

Harnwell, G. P. The world's problems have become the university's problems. *The Pennsylvania Gazette,* 1966, 65, 6–27.

Human Resources Center, University of Pennsylvania. *A report to President Gaylord P. Harnwell on University of Pennsylvania employment policy in the construction trades.* Philadelphia: Institute for Environmental Studies, 1969.

Jacob, P. E. *Changing values in college.* New York: Harper & Brothers, 1957.

Klotsche, J. M. *The urban university and the future of our cities.* New York: Harper & Row, 1966.

Mallery, D. *Ferment on the campus: An encounter with the new college generation.* New York: Harper & Row, 1966.

Marris, P., & Rein, M. *Dilemmas of social reform.* New York: Atherton Press, 1967.

Mitchell, H. E. The psychologist and society: One man's adventure into community psychology. In D. Adelson and B. Kalis (Eds.), *Community psychology and mental health.* Scranton, Pa.: Chandler, 1970.

Sanford, Nevitt. Whatever happened to action research? *Journal of Social Issues,* 26, 1970, 3–23.

Urban Institute. *A directory of university urban research centers.* Washington, D. C.: Urban Institute, 1969.

Warren, R. P. *Who speaks for the Negro?* New York: Vintage, 1966.

Wildavsky, A. Black rebellion and white reaction. *The Public Interest,* 1968, 11, 3–16.

4. Developing Indigenous Community Leadership: A Challenge to Urban Universities

EDWARD E. CAHILL
YVONNE SCRUGGS PERRY

INTRODUCTION

The advent of various pieces of social legislation during the 1960's presented a strong challenge to urban universities. Notable among these legislative programs were the Economic Opportunity Act of 1964 and the Demonstration Cities and Metroplitan Development Act of 1966 (Model Cities).[1] However, the challenge—that of drawing upon the wealth of existing and documented knowledge of leadership behavior, management techniques, and the systematic analysis of problems in working with impoverished or very low-income communities in cities—was by and large shunned by universities and their faculties.[2] A disorganized or altogether nonexistent reference to past

[1] The Higher Education Act of 1965 and amendments to various existing authorizations to Federal departments such as Labor and HUD augmented resources for leadership development at many levels also.
[2] The Upward Bound program was an exception (see Levitan, 1965, 1969).

experience and learning in community mobilization characterized many projects funded by the new legislation, and doomed them to limited success from the outset. Insufficient financial and human resources (Sundquist, 1969; Levitan, 1969; Moynihan, 1969), political intrigues, parallel structures (Moynihan, 1969; Piven and Cloward, 1971; Sundquist, 1969; Levitan, 1969), and a failure to recognize the importance of developing techniques of leadership and management in indigent communities[3] (Moynihan, 1969) were weaknesses that could not be overcome by administrative fiat.

While many universities and colleges were capable of developing leadership potential, comparatively few were willing to assume the burden of initiating programs and following the Guidelines requiring cooperation with Community Action Agencies. There were, of course, some individuals and small groups of faculty members at some institutions of higher learning who visualized more active involvement of such institutions beyond a purely academic level of study, research, and teaching youths from poverty backgrounds. Syracuse University, Wayne State University, Case Institute, and the University of Wisconsin had faculty groups committed to this expanded approach. The Graduate School of Social Work, Center for the Study of Unemployed Youth of New York University and the University of Chicago School of Social Work cooperated in the Midway Project.[4] Adelphi, Fordham, Hunter College, and New York and Yeshiva Universities joined with Mobilization for Youth in a program of training (Beck, 1969). The College of Medicine of Ohio State University, the University of Kentucky, and two other educational institutions (Kadish, 1969) had, by 1969, developed programs to assist communities in their use of the

[3]The language of the Economic Opportunity Act called for "maximum feasible participation" without seeking to define it or establish guidelines.
[4]For a full discussion of New York University's program, see Schmais, 1967.

social legislation. However, these examples of university response are few in number when compared with the volume increase during that decade in participation by residents of indigent communities, many of whom universities could have assisted.

Recognizing that the legislative programs of the 1960's had brought about increased demands on indigenous leadership and that this leadership often was of uneven quality and capability, the Human Resources Center (HRC) of the University of Pennsylvania initiated a program in 1970 which attempted to respond to these observations. This program, called the Community Leadership Seminar, was an action-research effort to improve the skills and increase the knowledge base of leaders in indigenous Philadelphia communities, a few with which HRC had cooperated previously.[5] This article reports on that program and states some implications for further university participation with indigent communities in their problem-solving processes.

PRECEDENTS FOR UNIVERSITY INTERVENTION

Universities, colleges, and institutions of higher education in general have distinguished themselves historically as incubators for talented women and men. These men and women, trained in the objectivity of the scientific method, have been and are now viewed as potential leaders in their respective disciplines and professions. Moreover, because they possess an academic degree, they constitute a major portion of the "leadership resources" to which frequent public reference is made. Their image is one at least of *potential* leadership, complete with general skills, trained perceptions, and "know-how." Historically, therefore, the development of leadership qualities has been one imperative of higher education.

[5]See Mitchell's article in this volume.

In recent years universities, particularly those located in urban settings, have broadened their resources and horizons in a manner which might be described as social opportunism.[6] Universities have recognized community leaders as part of the process by which students are trained. The successful business, medical, or industrial leader frequently enjoys the post of adjunctive professor, offering his experiential skills in the context of a conceptualized and structured learning setting. He teaches that which he has learned from his achievement of success. As he participates in the educational process within the university, he reflects the university's focus on leadership, as a goal as well as a resource.

Guest lecturers also are commonly drawn from a leadership class which exists external to the university. The social and behavioral sciences are frequent users of this leadership resource, as are performing and fine arts departments.

In yet another way, leaders from the community-at-large establish liaison with the university; they have found it to be a comfortable setting for peer-level conferences, workshops, and symposia. Simultaneously, they draw on the skills of faculty who act as resources for the dialogue. In this situation the university *and* the conferees benefit from a mutual reinforcement process: the leaders are recognized for their status and expertise, and the university fulfills its educational goal of contributing to and sustaining leadership growth.

Universities have also engaged in other types of non-credit training to develop leadership. Special training for management personnel, for example, has long been an accepted practice in schools of business and finance within colleges and universities. Civic leadership training, under the encouragement and financial support from the

[6]For a somewhat critical appraisal of this opportunism, see Sowell, 1970.

business and civic community, also has been developed in academic settings. Programs such as one conducted by the Fels Institute of Local and State Government of the University of Pennsylvania, have sought to increase the quality and quantity of civic leadership resources at a very broadly defined community level. Begun in 1959, this project at the Fels Institute was designed to

> strengthen community life in the Philadelphia area.
> ... Able young executives and outstanding knowl-
> edgeable persons qualified to discuss major metro-
> politan area problems were ... brought together in
> intensive seminar discussions. The general philoso-
> phy on which the program is based recognizes that
> a gap exists too often between government and the
> vast number of citizens it is created to serve. This gap
> has been bridged in part by private leadership
> groups representing a wide variety of commercial,
> industrial, social and religious interests. (Fels Insti-
> tute, 1966).

Thus the precedent for leadership training and rein-forcement through the university has long been recognized for those who have been given the opportunities of higher education.

For those less fortunate, but nonetheless called upon to be community leaders by the forces of circumstances in which they found themselves, similar training opportunities had not been presented. Acting upon its experience and previous research (Biddle, 1965; Bruyn, 1963; King, 1965; Mezirow, 1963), HRC hypothesized that

> urban communities have fallen short in the achieve-
> ment of their goals not only because of inadequacy of
> funds in implementing programs, but because of the
> failure or inability of community leadership groups
> to plan, program and manage their assets in the best
> possible manner to achieve their goals (Perry and
> Cahill, 1971).

The collective community experience of HRC staff had demonstrated that there were many "natural" adult leaders in impoverished communities. Often their leadership capabilities were rendered sterile in dealing with the larger community powers because of lack of knowledge, sophistication, and ability to articulate goals into program proposals which could be both manageable and funded. These same leaders might never benefit from college or university training because their previous formal educational development had been inadequate to meet entry standards established by colleges and universities. For others, the cost of continued education had been prohibitive. Yet, these men and women were community leaders today, however ill-prepared by academic standards.

THE COMMUNITY LEADERSHIP SEMINAR: STUDY AND PROGRAM

In an attempt to develop a better relationship with and knowledge of indigent communities and their problems, the Human Resources Center engaged in a project with leaders from a number of communities in the Philadelphia area. The indigenous community leadership project (formally known as The Community Leadership Seminar) was designed to be both a pilot study and a program for working with leaders and/or potential leaders living in areas characterized as blighted or deteriorating. It was to:

1) identify existing or potential community leaders capable of effectuating constructive changes in their communities;
2) invite these leaders, not to exceed thirty in number, to participate in and plan a program to include:
    a) the definition of realizable goals, in housing, medical services, recreational facilities, community maintenance, etc.,

  b) techniques for achieving goals, in housing, medical services, recreational facilities, community maintenance, etc.,

  c) basic principles of business management and systematized bookkeeping,

  d) techniques of proposal writing,

  e) communications techniques and interpersonal relations,

  f) other areas at the discretion of the participants;

3) draw on the resources of the University and established channels in the city to work with these leaders for more effective communication, social change, and improvement of the human condition in the city of Philadelphia;

4) establish continuing mechanisms for leadership training in community organization that would be both responsive to the communities' needs and responsible to legitimate authorities and funding sources;

5) involve students in city planning, community organization or other allied fields in the program so that they might learn to work more closely and positively with indigenous community leaders after the initial program became operational. (Perry and Cahill, 1971).

It was designed also to try to learn from these leaders how the University might serve best the needs of these communities while maintaining its continuing goals of increasing knowledge through scholarly research and of communicating that knowledge (Human Resources Center, 1970). Finally, the objective was not merely to "have a program" for indigenous community leaders, but to plan a program *with* them. Thus, their perceived needs would be met while the University learned from them ways in which it might explore and develop further its own resources to improve the quality of life in urban areas.

Implementing the project toward these ends required consensus of the project staff on two basic criteria; that the leadership to participate in the program must represent existing organizations, and that these organizations would be selected from the areas known as the "inner-city" areas. Hopefully, a multiplier effect would then take place among a broad-based representation of community leaders already working in established community organizations. The participants would bring the real problems with which they had to contend to the Seminar. University staff would work with them both individually and collectively. Thus the project would psychically support the participant in his continuing analysis of actions taken and the rationale for such action.

SELECTION OF PARTICIPANTS

An initial survey enumerating existing community organizations in the designated geographic area was conducted. Key figures[7] from a list of well-known professional administrators of city-wide community development programs were interviewed. They were asked to identify organizations which might participate in this project, basing their recommendations on four criteria:

1) The organizations should be fairly well established and give promise of continuing in existence for at least another year.
2) Their geographic locations should require that they have important problems with which to copo, i.e., they should not be in settled, isolated communities.

[7]Based on a concept developed by Irwin Sanders and Peter Rossi in memos to the Community Renewal Program in Philadelphia, and found in variation in Bell, *et al.*, 1961, and Charles M. Bonjean, "Class, Status and Power Reputation," *Sociology and Social Research*, 49, 1964.

3) Their membership should be large enough in number to include emergent as well as recognized leadership among its ranks.
4) The organizations should be able to benefit from such a training program, in the opinion of the Key Figure.

Thirty-six organizations were identified in this manner. Through refining criteria to give balance to participation on the bases of geographic location, racial composition of organizations, and perceived need, twenty organizations were invited to send representatives to the initial planning of the program and the follow-up study.[8]

The twenty participants were generally officers, or chairmen of task forces or committees of their respective organizations. They were between the ages of 30 and 45, with dependent children, and had resided in the areas of their auspice organization for ten or more years. About half (42%) had not completed high school, but five had attended or completed college. Only one participant was unemployed, while the others represented a wide variety of occupations from skilled craftsmen to school teachers.

Seminar Structure

Previous experience with adult leadership programs[9] led the seminar faculty to plan the twelve weekly sessions "with" the participants rather than "for" them. Thus the content from the outset ensured greater participation and interest because it reflected a group decision.

The seminar topics finally agreed upon included:

[8]A more complete description of the organizational characteristics and those of the individual participants are contained in Perry and Cahill, 1971, pp. 18–37.

[9]The Human Resources Center had previously engaged in adult leadership programs with other groups in Philadelphia, 1967–68, and with a group of suburban leaders seeking information on urban problems. Also see Mitchell, 1965; Bee, 1969; and Zurcher, 1970.

1) A general understanding of social systems;
2) The nature and functions of the economic system;
3) Political structure and government funding;
4) Elements of community organization and gang control;
5) The role of private foundations in solving community problems;
6) The search for funds and mechanisms of applying for them;
7) Techniques of proposal writing and responsibilities to funding sources;
8) Interplay of private funding and governmental support in community activities;
9) Problems of physical rehabilitation of communities;
10) Reducing problems to manageable size;
11) Techniques and problems of strengthening community organizations;
12) Roles and responsibilities of established specific governmental agencies at all levels in dealing with community problems.

The number of seminars was affected both by the initial limitations of funds for developing the pilot program and by the expressed desires of the participants. Originally HRC staff thought two seminars of two hours each week would provide the basis for a sound beginning program. Participants rejected this, however, in view of other commitments which they had and the exigencies of getting to the University from a distance. It was finally agreed to conduct twelve weekly seminars of two-and-a-half hours length in this initial phase.

EVALUATION

To a few, some elements of the seminar sessions were redundant, but generally the knowledge acquired there and in the discussions of each evening were a good indication of the learning which occurred. This is reflected in the evaluation of each session given by the respondents[10] (Perry and Cahill, 1971). On a five-point evaluative scale, ranging from "Useless" to "Very Helpful," no more than two responses for any one session were rated either "Useless" of "Of Limited Value." To the contrary, the normal pattern indicated all sessions were either "Very Helpful" or "Helpful" to more than 85% of those who attended them.

SIX-MONTH FOLLOW-UP EVALUATION

The original proposal called for a follow-up evaluation both of the seminars and of action taken in the community following participation in the program. While there had been considerable community-related activity by the participants, the six-month follow-up evaluation proved to be too soon to note significant changes resulting from participation in the Community Leadership Seminar at the University. Moreover, the lack of adequate knowledge of the individual participant's activity in his auspice community organization prior to participation in the Seminar precluded the possibility of graphic measurement after participation. Generally, however, participants indicated that the University-based seminars were very helpful to them, particularly in learning where they should go to obtain answers to fundamental questions, and for funds and support for solutions to localized programs. More specifically, participants indicated both an

[10]A complete description of the techniques used for analysis and evaluation is contained in Perry and Cahill, 1971. The test of effectiveness lies principally in major behavioral changes that were manifested by the participants in their work in the community. Unfortunately, the seminars were begun before an adequate assessment of the existing situation could be made for each individual.

increased knowledge in attacking community problems and a confidence of approach that they had not previously experienced (Perry and Cahill, 1971).

CONCLUSIONS

From the outset of the Community Leadership Seminar, critical voices were raised within the University as well as within outside community organizations concerning the propriety of conducting such a program in the University. Internal to the University were the usual questions of a university-based unit providing a kind of service for communities without having the financial or political resources to solve community problems directly. "Was this not just another case of a university raising the hopes of already indigent communities without being able to fulfill them?"

External to the University, questions were raised by a number of persons regarding the "motives" of the University's involvement. Indeed, this question of "credibility" arose frequently from the participants themselves. The staff, both individually and collectively, were frequently "tested" by the participants to determine their sincerity.

The evidence in the end supported the faith expressed in the original proposal. There is a pronounced status advantage to community leaders in having sessions in the relative neutrality of a university classroom setting, in having staff capable of approaching problems with the objectivity of scientists evoking practical solutions to human concerns, and in having the experience of teaching techniques that elude many in dealing with classroom management-type problems. The relatively neutral base of the University caused the participants to examine the issues confronting them rather than to attack the persons presenting the issues. The question therefore becomes

"Who can handle such a learning situation better?" Certainly not governmental agencies, which tend to become defensive about the limited resources which they have at their disposal and the value-priorities used in distributing them. And certainly not the individual community, where the problem may be so intensely felt and steeped in emotion that even the coolest heads may not prevail.

That the university is a logical base for developing indigenous leaders was confirmed by the respondents themselves. They answered the question dealing with how the university could be most helpful to organizations involved in community work as follows:

1) by continuing its educative function through extending the seminars and remaining in contact with the organizations attending the seminars;
2) providing material, references, back-up, etc., to planned programs;
3) becoming a source for information that is not commonly available to indigenous community people—not doing the work for them, but extending aid so they can more easily solve their problems;
4) training people to understand terminology of proposal writing and contracts;
5) conducting classes to train people for specialized work;
6) open the College to more Black students;
7) starting motivation classes for advanced education for community workers; and
8) letting community workers have access to university resources of personnel and knowledge. (Perry and Cahill, 1971).

Without equivocation, there is a value to the program herein described. Such study and research challenges urban universities today, *viz.*, visibility and accessibility to the downtrodden communities which exist in their penumbra almost everywhere. The question is less whether or not it should be done than how it can be most effectively accomplished.[11]

Much of the knowledge necessary to successful achievement of specific community goals is available at colleges and universities in a variety of disciplines, albeit widely diffused. Or, if not readily available among members of the faculty and adjunct personnel, at least the knowledge of where to go to find necessary resources usually is present. Thus the college or university may play a significant role in developing indigenous community leaders through the knowledge it communicates, its points of contact in the existing social structure, and its techniques for communication.

On the other hand, universities, their administrators and faculty, have much to learn from impoverished communities regarding such things as style of life, reasons and causes of impoverishment, modes of communication, meaning of symbols, patterns of adjustment, etc. It is both striking and alarming to find universities, housing world-renowned institutes of "other cultures" from other continents, whose staff know very little of the cultural patterns, problems, and life-styles of the very communities in which they reside. It is disheartening to see scholars, often able to speak many foreign languages, unable to communicate with the people a few blocks away from the campus because they have not taken the time to learn the nuances of language, gestures, and symbols that would create understanding and mutual respect.

Scholars have devoted far too little attention to the historical roots and causes of problems within their immediate social environment. Professors often achieve university support for exotic studies far removed in time, space, and social distance with greater facility than those with serious intent and scholarly concern who are desirous of

[11]The Community Leadership Seminar has since been replicated, in 1972 and 1973, by the Human Resources Center. This replication, the Urban Leadership Seminar, involved 30 organizations, divided into two phases, each meeting for a 10- to 12-week period.

studying and working with people and their problems within walking distance of urban universities. It seems to be easier to generalize about national or international problems of racism than to deal with problems of poverty, blight, and destruction of both environment and people in the communities immediately surrounding many urban universities. In so complicated an area of concern as human development in an urban setting, scientific methods are too often abandoned and instant experts without sufficient scholarly concern gain ascendancy.

Although scholarly works dealing with some of the aforementioned problems are increasing in number (Liebow, 1967; Moore, 1969; McCord, *et al.*, 1969), the majority of publications dealing with these problems tend to be either too general for scholarly application or too specific for general application. Perhaps, for some segments of the university at least, the time has come to encourage the principles of scholarship in local areas, directly applicable to those areas, limited though it may be in achieving national or international fame for the sponsoring institution. Scholars thus involved would necessarily have to be rated against a set of criteria different from many of those currently applicable in major urban universities. Nonetheless, they must be recognized and promoted, with long-overdue respect for the critical importance of their work in solving urban problems.

We concur with The Assembly on University Goals and Governance, which states:

> The problems of instruction today are different from what they were a decade ago; they are likely to become even more different if the theses with respect to access and certification suggested above, are realized. ... Modernity may best be studied on two levels: what unites the planet and what divides it. ... The spiritual and material fantasies of our time cannot be disassociated from their roots. The concern must be with interpreting and understanding modern man's political and social predicament, seeing

these in a context that takes account of his psychic and spiritual needs. (The American Academy of Arts and Sciences, 1971).

There is a continuing imperative for universities to face the challenges presented by poverty in urban areas. Universities possess resources which have been neither developed in this regard nor used wisely in the past. The objectivity, scholarly concern, and initiative which prevail in the academic contribution to developing other areas of leadership must prevail also in the development of indigenous community leadership.

REFERENCES

The American Academy of Arts and Sciences. *A first report: The assembly on university goals and governance.* Cambridge: The American Academy of Arts and Sciences, 1971.

The Annals of the American Academy of Political and Social Sciences. Evaluating the War on Poverty. L. Ferman, Ed. Philadelphia: The American Academy of Political and Social Science, 1969.

Beck, B. Non-professional social work personnel. In C. Grosser, W. E. Henry, and J. G. Kelly (Eds.), *Non-professionals in the human services.* San Francisco: Jossey-Bass, Inc., 1969.

Bee, R. L. Tribal leadership in war on poverty. *Social Science Quarterly,* December 1969, (50), 3.

Bell, W., *et al. Public leadership: A critical review with special reference to adult education.* San Francisco: Chandler Publishing Co., 1961.

Biddle, W. W. and L. J. *The community development process.* New York: Holt, Rinehart and Winston, Inc., 1965.

Bruyn, S. T. *Communities in action.* New Haven: College and University Press, 1963.

Fels Institute of Local and State Government. *Metropolitan area problems with particular reference to Philadelphia.* Philadelphia: University of Pennsylvania, 1966.

Human Resources Center. A pilot program for indigenous community leadership training. Mimeographed proposal, 1970.

Human Resources Program: A summary of the first two years 1964–1966. Philadelphia: University of Pennsylvania, 1966.

Kadish, J. Programs in the federal government. In C. Grosser, *et al.* (Eds.), *Non-professionals in the human services.* San Francisco: Jossey-Bass, Inc., 1969.

King, C. *Working with people in community action.* New York: Association Press, 1965.

Levitan, S. A. The community action program: A strategy to fight poverty. *The Annals of the American Academy of Political and Social Science:* Evaluating the War on Poverty. Sept. 1969, pp. 63–75.

Levitan, S. A. *The great society's poor law.* Baltimore: The Johns Hopkins Press, 1969.

Levitan, S. A. *Upward bound: Policy guidelines and application instructions.* Washington, D. C.: Community Action Program, 1965.

Liebow, E. *Tally's corner.* Boston: Little, Brown and Co., 1967.

McCord, W., *et al. Life styles in the black ghetto.* New York: W. W. Norton and Co., Inc., 1969.

Mezirow, J. D. *Dynamics of community development.* New York: Scarecrow Press, 1963.

Mitchell, H. E. *A summer residential educational project for culturally deprived youth.* Philadelphia: Human Resources Center, 1965.

Moore, W., Jr. *The vertical ghetto: Everyday life in an urban project.* New York: Random House, 1969.

Moynihan, D. P. *Maximum feasible misunderstanding: Community action in the war on poverty.* New York: The Free Press, 1969.

Perry, Y. S., and Cahill, E. E. *The community leadership seminar: A report on a university-community joint venture.* Philadelphia: Human Resources Center, University of Pennsylvania, 1971.

Piven, F. F., and Cloward, R. A. *Regulating the poor: The functions of public welfare.* New York: Pantheon Books, 1971.

Schmais, A. *Implementing non-professional programs in human services.* New York University Graduate School of Social Work, Center for the Study of Unemployed Youth, 1967.

Sowell, T. The available university. *University of Chicago Magazine,* December 1970.

Sundquist, J. L. Coordinating the war on poverty. *The Annals of the American Academy of Political and Social Science:* Evaluating the War on Poverty. September 1969, pp. 41–49.

U. S. Office of Economic Opportunity. *Community action workbook.* Washington: Office of Economic Opportunity, Section III A7, 1965.

Zurcher, L. A., Jr. *Poverty warriors: The human experience of planned intervention.* Austin: University of Texas Press, 1970.

5. A New Partnership for Social Change: The Urban University and Suburban Women

MARTHA LAVELL

In recent years there have been innumerable publications concerned with the changing role of women. Many cite the increasing numbers of women in the labor force, and the resultant problems in combining marriage and a career. Some writers, however, advocate a career for every mother or at least career training for young women in the event that they will need or desire to go to work at a later date (Myrdal, 1968).

Agnes E. Meyer (1962) points out that marriage has become only a part-time career for women, demanding their full attention for less than one-third of adult life. Yet the highest proportion of women in the labor force is no more than 56% at ages 20—24 and 54% at ages 45—54 (Suelze, 1970). If childrearing and housekeeping duties are now of a part-time nature but nearly half of American women are unemployed, how are they spending their time? A considerable number are doing volunteer work; there are endless opportunities of this kind, primarily in the delivery of services. These tend to be specific tasks aimed at important but narrow goals.[1]

[1]There has been no national census of volunteers. Around 8.5 million are reported to be serving through agencies associated with the United Community Funds and Councils of America. The National School Volunteer Program engages the efforts of 200,000 volunteers (Shaffer, 1969).

Nevitt Sanford (1967) has suggested a different role for women: looking after whole communities. "Our greatest tasks at the present time have to do with the development and improvement of people, with the expansion and enrichment of their lives, with the improvement of their relations one to another, and with the development and maintenance of communities in which these things are possible . . ." Sanford believes the helping professions are not adequate to these tasks; instead he calls for "a vast army of generally educated women, 'subprofessional,' as is sometimes said, who can and will turn their hands to almost anything, who would constitute a sort of 'third force,' as it were, and who, free of professional constraints, could move into situations where there was special need." This possibility was also noted by the Committee on Education of the President's Commission on the Status of Women (1963). In a section on education for volunteering, the report suggested that "more thought should be given to the education and utilization of the 'generalist' in the community—that person who is able to cut across many disciplines and spark new solutions to troubling problems."

University continuing-education programs have for the past ten years performed a useful function in providing opportunities for women long out of school to resume their education with career or job goals in mind. Programs for education of volunteers have received less attention by educational institutions, in spite of a recommendation by the above-mentioned committee. Sanford's further thoughts on this matter are pertinent: The third-force women "would have to be continuously educated—in situations and by techniques that have not as yet been worked out. One thing seems certain: there would be no great point in their going back to school, to sit among budding professionals learning academic specialties. Instead, they should organize themselves into action groups and insist that the university come to them, through professors who had something to contribute to-

ward solving the genuine problems that were being attacked."

A beginning has been made along these lines in an ·
experimental program at the Human Resources Center,
University of Pennsylvania. Developed at the request of
Penn alumnae who were concerned about urban problems and the cleavages in American society, and partially
funded under Title I of the Higher Education Act of 1965,
it aims to equip housewives with the skills they need to
become agents of change in their suburban communities.
As offered during 1969 and 1970 it attracted altogether 54
women, most of whom completed the 30 sessions com-
prising the program. The following report describes the
program, the participants, the outcome, and implications
for the University and the urban condition.

Recruitment took place in three ways: through the
Alumnae Association, through the Junior League of Philadelphia, and by word of mouth. Since interest was greater
than had been anticipated, a larger number of applicants
(26) was accepted the first year than had been planned.
Since this number proved to be too large, in the program
as repeated in 1970 the women were divided into two
groups, of 12 and 16 members, meeting on different days.

The program consisted of 30 weekly sessions with a
hiatus over the summer. Sessions lasted from two to two
and one-half hours. Subject matter included basic material in urban problems, the nature of prejudice, governmental budgets and priorities, theory of planned change,
urban-suburban relationships, group behavior and the
handling of conflict, black militance and white reaction,
and problems of institutional change. Four sessions on
group dynamics were concerned with effective listening,
achieving consensus, recognition of individual strengths
and weaknesses, and the constructive expression of negative feelings. It was felt that development of these skills
would be more useful than any emphasis on in-depth
group experience. Staff deliberately avoided "encounter"
and "sensitivity training" designs that would encourage

the women to examine their own or each other's psychodynamics.

The format of the regular sessions included, besides lectures and discussion, some role playing, films, reports by trainees on topics of special interest which they had studied independently under staff guidance, and some preliminary reports on trainee activities in their own communities. Prior to the last mentioned, each trainee had participated in a small-group discussion with the coordinator of trainees, for mutual exploration of feasible avenues of action. During the 1970 program, the trainees in the two separate groups met together on one occasion in a housing workshop. Both years a dinner meeting with a prominent change agent as a speaker offered opportunity for husbands to have some contact with program and staff.

Supportive materials were supplied at each session: pamphlets, magazine or newspaper articles, graphs and tabular data, summaries of studies, excerpts from books, and reprints and reports. In the 1970 program, *Institutional Racism in America,* by Knowles and Prewitt, was used as basic reading. A special learning experience each year was provided by field trips which gave first-hand knowledge of conditions in the Philadelphia ghetto and the indigenous community organizations working to improve them.

Human Resources Center staff, which is interdisciplinary, bore the main teaching load throughout the program but were supplemented by various resource persons. These included a lawyer active in a community legal services endeavor; an official from the Welfare Department; a member of an activist suburban church; a psychologist in charge of a program to explore discriminatory policies, practices, and procedures in industry; indigenous community leaders with special interest and experiences; and a staff member of a prison reform organization.

Throughout the program, staff was available to the trainees for consultation on program content and techniques for use in their endeavors. After the formal program terminated, this relationship continued through 1970 for the participants in the first year's program. In addition, they were encouraged to share their experiences with the participants in the second year. The 1971 program, which was conceived as a supportive service to former trainees who wished to pass on to other women what they had learned, will be described in the section on outcome.

THE PARTICIPANTS

For ease in presentation, detailed description will be confined to the first year's trainees.[2] Sources of data were the application form and a questionnaire completed by the trainees concerning their experiences, their knowledge of urban problems and civil rights, and their special concerns.

In only a few ways was this a homogeneous group: all except two trainees were unemployed married women with children, all were white women, and 77% were college graduates. They ranged in age from the twenties to the fifties, and annual family income ranged from $10,000 to $100,00 (median around $30,000). Their places of residence were in both the near suburbs and the far suburbs (15 to 20 miles out from Philadelphia), with a small number residing in some suburban-like areas within the city. The trainees also exhibited a great range of experience and knowledge. Half of them had been involved in civil rights activities of various kinds. Some had worked for fair housing or better human relations. Two had participated in demonstrations against discriminatory practices. The

---

[2]Trainees in the second year did not differ greatly except that they included three Negro women.

Poor People's March, the Welfare Rights cause, a black-white confrontation series, the Panel of Philadelphians (local chapter of the Panel of American Women), writing articles on the urban crisis for a club paper, were other activities mentioned.

All but four women had done some reading in the fields of civil rights, race relations, or urban problems. The exact extent of this reading is not known. What stands out is the fact that, although a total of 33 books was mentioned, only four books had been read by more than three women. These were the Kerner Commission Report, read in part or in whole by 15 women; the *Autobiography of Malcolm X*, read by 10 women; Cleaver's *Soul on Ice* by eight women; and Silberman's *Crisis in Black and White* by seven women. Another significant point is that, of the 22 women who reported some books read, 21 had read one or more of the above books. All four are contemporary publications that received considerable attention in the mass media; the vast literature predating 1964 has evidently not been generally available to or read by the trainees.

A very general index of the level of knowledge of the trainees in the area of civil rights is available. There was a great range apparent, and the knowledge was uneven. Some examples will illustrate: At least two-thirds of the group knew that Negroes had served in American wars prior to World War II, and that research generally shows that Negroes in racially mixed classrooms do better on achievement tests than do Negroes from similar family backgrounds who are in segregated classrooms. On the other hand, only 54% were aware that discrimination because of race by private employers is specifically forbidden under federal law, and only 50% knew that Edward W. Brooke was not the first Negro to be elected to the U.S. Senate. The trainees generally exaggerated the percentage of nonwhite families on welfare nationwide, with some estimates over 70%, and they underestimated the percentage of nonwhite families that are structurally intact, with some estimates under 20%. One may conclude from these data that the trainees had not been spared the myths and stereotypes afflicting many white persons in American society. In light of this fact, it is noteworthy that this was a group of women concerned about urban problems and open to new knowledge and concepts.

The reasons given by trainees for applying for the program demonstrated their concern and showed little range. Fifteen trainees mentioned a desire to contribute toward the solution of urban problems; six replies could be categorized as awareness of need for factual information, four as awareness of need for skills to become more effective; and five trainees felt the program would be useful in their current endeavors. Typical answers: "I am terribly anxious to change the conditions of our society that permit racism and discrimination and exploitation to exist." "I hope to learn *how* to bring about change." "I would like facts in order to learn where I and my friends can help." "I need to develop skill in discussing the problems ..." "... to use the information and techniques of the program in the areas where I am already working."

That some of the women felt a lack of confidence in their own abilities was apparent early in the program. Though open to action suggestions, they were reluctant to act individually; some showed interest in acting as a group by forming small discussion panels. The trainees often commented on the support they obtained from each other, from the Center staff, and from being affiliated in this way with the University.

At midpoint in the program 23 trainees indicated in which areas they felt their talents could be effectively used as agents of change. This self-assessment, though possibly affected by the five month program experience, may offer a picture of some value. Two areas were checked more than any others: interpreting urban problems to friends or family (18 trainees) and encouraging institutional change (16 trainees). Nine trainees felt they could recruit interested persons to offer service to ghetto enterprises; nine checked the area, making contact with key officials to demonstrate their concern. Seven were interested in helping to reduce intergroup tensions. Only four felt their talents were in the area of leading group discussions on urban problems. Two trainees checked "Not certain" on this question and one checked "Other," specifying as follows: "trying to move groups from within, not as a leader but pushing leaders."

OUTCOME

In evaluating the program, staff has relied heavily on trainee reports of their activities and attitude changes. The data so far gathered are subjective and incomplete, since the effects of a program of this kind can be vague and long-range. It was obvious throughout the two years' program that the trainees were at different points in their receptivity to new ideas and their readiness to act. It may take more time and more experience for some trainees to identify their talents as agents of change and to find avenues of action in which they feel secure. Some, indeed, may not reach this point.

Outcome data to be reported are of three kinds; (a) evaluation questionnaire responses by trainees at midpoint or at close of program, (b) reports of activities from 18 women in the first-year group at various times during the program and at a point six to eight months after the program ended, and (c) a description of the involvement of 24 trainees in efforts to train or activate others under a cluster-group structure provided by the Center in 1971.

Evaluation by Trainees

That the program had an effect on the trainees' self-image was apparent from questionnaire data at the midpoint of the program for the 1969 trainees and at the close of the program for the 1970 group. Nineteen of 23 trainees (82.6%) reporting in June 1969 said their view of themselves had changed: 15 as an individual, 14 as a community member, 11 as a member of a social group, and 8 as a family member. (Two were not certain and two did not answer the question.) In December 1970, 21 of 24 trainees reporting said their view of themselves had changed: 16 as an individual, 16 as a community member, 9 as a member of a social group, and 9 as a family member. (Three gave a negative reply.) These findings were consistent from one year to the next.

At the midpoint in 1969, of the 23 trainees reporting, 18 offered comments pertaining to such effects as a heightened commitment or sense of urgency (6 persons), an increased awareness of their own or others' needs or goals or potential (6 persons), an experience of being more effective (3 persons), and an increased confidence (3 persons).

At the close of the program, four-fifths of the 1969 group and two-thirds of the 1970 group reported they felt they were more effective in their endeavors as a result of the program.

The 1970 trainees at the close of the program offered a wide array of changes in attitude or action as a result of the program; most prominent among these were a better grasp or use of techniques (33%), a more committed or responsible feeling (25%), a less critical, more open-minded attitude (25%), and an increased readiness to speak up (21%).

Activities of the First-Year Trainees

Sanford referred in an apt phrase to women "who can and will turn their hands to almost anything." What are the kinds of activities to which the 1969 trainees turned their attention? These were sometimes new avenues of action; in other cases they represented a focusing or concentrating in areas of prior interest with the use of new ideas or techniques. Activities are of three types: efforts to educate, activate, or change, with varying targets; efforts to help individuals or groups in the ghetto; and efforts to educate themselves further by investigation. Some actions are purely individual, some in cooperation with friends and associates.

The church constitutes a most natural avenue of action for some women; ten trainees became involved in efforts to educate their fellow church members or arouse them to action. Educational programs employing a variety of techniques and topics; interdenominational exploration of similarities and differences toward the goal of increased mutual understanding; and a variety of social action efforts—such are the opportunities under church auspices.

Suburban schools are also a fertile area for change agents. The eleven women who focused on school actions had three related purposes in view: (1) the fostering of intergroup understanding so as to improve human relations in the school itself,[3] (2) changing or improving the school curriculum toward more adequate treatment of minorities and their contribution to American culture, or toward better coverage of social problems, and (3) changing discriminatory or repressive practices in the schools.

Many women are members of organizations that are open to or in need of change; ten women in this program reported actions focused on such organizations as private clubs, a doctors' wives group, the Junior League, the American Association of University Women, a community association, and a book-reading club. The actions varied from program suggestions to pressures for admissions policy changes.

Suburban women in the Philadelphia area have traditionally served on boards and committees of social and civic agencies. The pressures for change have not left

[3]Some suburban schools in the Philadelphia area have Jewish-Gentile tensions, often unacknowledged by administrators; others with a small Negro minority in their student bodies are experiencing some conflict.

these agencies untouched, and six of the trainees have endeavored to interpret the pressures and to encourage institution of new policies and procedures toward the more humane and equitable provision of services. One example is inclusion of minority group members on boards.

Exerting pressure on government agencies claimed the attention of six women. This took various forms: discussions with legislators regarding welfare reform, demonstrations at the state capitol, interviews with police officials, participation in a study of police-community relations which resulted in a public resolution, meetings with township commissioners regarding re-zoning, acting as watchdog for a redevelopment and a housing authority, and marching in a picket line around City Hall in an effort to get funds appropriated for gang control and a lead poisoning program.

Business and industry are another possible target. Six trainees tried in various ways to influence employers to make constructive changes to encourage the hiring and promotion of Negro employees.

Other actions concerned with the general public rather than a specific target are as follows: working with fair housing groups or to promote low-income housing in the suburbs, serving on the board of an interfaith action group, working with a suburban human relations council, participating in conferences, planning a civic workshop, serving on the local affiliate of the Panel of American Women, stimulating a community group to study drug addiction, and supporting an American Friends Service Committee summer project attempting to modify racial prejudice.

Fifteen trainees have devoted some effort to helping individuals or groups in the Philadelphia ghetto in response to appeals from indigenous organizations. Their support in some cases has been merely financial, in others of a service nature. Included in the latter category were establishing a day care program, providing tutoring or recreational opportunities, and finding jobs or scholarships. One trainee has been a volunteer aide in an O.E.O. community action program.

In several ways the women sought further learning opportunities, for example by visiting the Juvenile Court and by attending conferences, such as one sponsored by the Welfare Rights organization and Community Services of Pennsylvania.

Trainees in Collaboration

During the year 1971 the Human Resources Center was able, again under partial Title I funding, to offer support to former trainees who wished to collaborate in educational or action programs. Five geographical cluster groups were set up, and programs planned and carried out, by 24 former trainees. These attracted around 150 newcomers. Four of the groups focused on education for action; their programs consisted of speakers, panels, discussions, and in one case some field trips. Topics covered a wide range of social problems. The fourth group decided on action, along with self-education, in the area of criminal justice. By visits to prisons, courts, prison board meetings, and social action agencies the participants laid the basis for becoming a pressure group for needed social change. Evidence of the group's impact began to accumulate in the latter part of 1971: a county prison board set up a citizens advisory council, a county commissioner saw the need for an advisory committee on prisons, a well-qualified woman was appointed to a prison board. The cluster group has continued to emphasize a search for alternatives to incarceration and is now attempting to arouse public sentiment against plans for a new but traditional-type county prison. The group is now functioning under the name "Main Line Cluster for Justice" and continues to attract new members.

The Human Resources Center has been a resource for all the cluster groups: providing some of the speakers, recommending materials, and offering some training in group participation skills. It encourages interaction between the cluster groups by setting up regular liaison meetings at the Center. Each cluster sends one or more representatives to the meetings, at which time informal reports on cluster programs are presented, problems are discussed, and decisions and recommendations made on matters affecting all cluster groups.

Although the Center's support had to be curtailed early in 1972, four of the cluster groups continued to function, including the action group mentioned above. Another group, in the Mt. Airy section of Philadelphia (which combines the amenities of suburban life with certain urban problems), saw a community need for a youth employment service and succeeded in establishing one. A third group began to look into action possibilities in the fields of drug education, problems of older adults, and criminal justice. The fourth cluster is now turning its attention to youth-adult relationships.

DISCUSSION

Throughout the three years of this program there have been two assumptions: that women in the suburbs constitute a largely unrealized human resource potential, and that the University's legitimizing function can be used to support social change. Both of these assumptions appear to have been justified. The effect of the program was to increase self-confidence and willingness to become actively involved in community problems, even to the extent of increased risk-taking. It was a common experience for the women to have doors opened to them because of their training. As one trainee put it, "People have heard about the course, ask about it, often rely on my suggestions and help, and consistently look to me for answers to specific questions."

As the program was originally planned it was seen, in the light of previous experience at the Center, as a training-of-trainers program. It was presumed that the women after training would be able to pass on to others what they had learned. In mainly informal ways, in contacts with family and associates, but also in program planning for organizations, this did indeed transpire. A more structured training by the trainees was realized in the 1971 cluster group program, as a result of planning by the Center rather than any need expressed by the trainees. As they proceeded to convene in geographical areas for planning they expressed considerable hesitancy about their own abilities to plan and carry out an education program and about the likelihood of community response. With staff support their doubts were reduced and their confidence increased.

One of the basic concepts in the program was that of the communication network. The cluster program added more units in a network diffusion of concepts, knowledge, and personal concern. As each member of a cluster is activated to influence her own community in her own way, additional units are added. For example, one member successfully planned two training programs for her church.[4] A problem of utilization of staff resources might arise if a considerable number of women developed interests in similar endeavors: for how much help can each trainee depend on the Center? It is advisable, therefore, that the responsibilities of the training agency toward trainees and also the "second generation" trained by them be carefully delineated. This necessitates consideration by academic staff of the question of in what way they can be most effective.

In the conduct of the program the staff found it necessary to maintain flexibility in planning and procedure. The original plan called for five sessions to present facts and theory as basic training. It became apparent that at least ten sessions were needed for this phase. Of the wide

---

[4]Although the term network is used here in its metaphorical sense (Mitchell, 1969) it is recognized that the expanding character of the social activist network offers singular research possibilities.

range of topics covered most met with interest and stimulated lively discussion. Though the informal discussion as well as the innumerable questions that were raised often interrupted a formal lecture, the time was considered by staff to have been well spent. Only a few women would have preferred to sacrifice the interchange for the more complete coverage of a subject that a formal uninterrupted lecture makes possible. Interaction between trainees and staff or resource persons, and also among trainees, provided an important source of learning. Two other fruitful techniques should be mentioned: the field trips, which had considerable impact, and the housing workshop in which most of the 1970 trainees participated. The latter offered opportunity for field investigation by the trainees into various aspects of the housing problem; the trainees worked individually or in small groups and then reported their findings to the entire workshop. Another indispensable element was the group skills training, to which only a few women reacted negatively. Most found the training very useful (a fact further attested to by the planning in the four educational cluster groups in 1971 for two or more sessions to be devoted to group participation skills). Some trainees said they would have liked the training earlier in the program because of its effect on the group itself: a group spirit developed which became a source of moral support to the participants.

A continuing emphasis has been on feedback from the trainees and the mutual learning that this permits. In the course of three years, gaps in staff awareness were decreased and new techniques were developed. The program was originally planned on the basis of knowledge of urban-suburban problems along with ignorance regarding suburban women—the level of their awareness and commitment, the type of sensitizing experiences they might have had, the range of activities they might engage in as nonprofessional women, and also the number of action groups already existing in the suburbs. During the 1969 program, data were accumulated on a rather disorganized basis which did remedy the ignorance sufficiently to permit more systematic data collection in 1970. One area of inquiry, however, presented special problems. In an attempt to set up a method of reporting of trainee activities it proved difficult to determine what actions should be reported and then to persuade the trainees to keep records of these actions. An improvement in the reporting form in 1970 brought some increase in the number of reports, but there is no way of telling whether no report from a particular trainee signified no activity. In addition, considerable difficulty was encountered in attempting to categorize action. There was indication of different orders of magnitude and an overlapping of units (e.g., serving on an action committee and participating in a committee action) so that a unit of action was difficult to isolate. (This problem seems similar to that of isolating units for content analysis of qualitative material throughout the social sciences.)

Three years' experience in this training program have led to the conceptualization of certain research questions that need systematic exploration. These pertain to the characteristics and role of women as change agents, to training techniques, and to strategies and arenas of action. It would be desirable to study what determines a woman's level of awareness or commitment, whether progression to the level of action is contingent upon a growth in willingness to take risks, and what factors contribute to such growth. In studying motivation, the appropriateness for this population of Barnett's typology of innovators might be investigated (Barnett, 1953). The question can be raised whether training techniques should differ depending on level of awareness.[5] A related question is whether

---

[5]In a study of the 1970 training group it was found that the less experienced trainees, when compared with those of more experience in social action, profited from different program elements and reached different levels of action at the close of the program (Lavell and Cahill).

heterogeneity of background provides learning experiences important enough to offset any disadvantages involved. Knowledge thus far gained about arenas and techniques of action for suburban women needs to be refined and expanded: what are the best pressure points, are some arenas more susceptible to impact, how can social action be measured? There are additional methodological questions having to do with the measurement of level of commitment and risk-taking readiness.

As the program developed successfully it became apparent that it could be viewed as a pilot program that could be fitted into the regular structure of the University in alternative ways, provided funding and commitment were forthcoming. Continuing education, as "a potent but underused weapon against social ills" (Knowles, 1970), constitutes a natural function of the University and could be performed on an expanded and formalized basis. The possibility has been explored at the University of Pennsylvania, with regard to a regular course in the College of General Studies, the extension arm of the University. Here enrollment would not be confined to women, since undergraduate students, particularly those going on to urban studies or city planning, might find the course useful. The resulting heterogeneity might enhance the value of the course (and even contribute to a narrowing of the generation gap!). A second possibility is a seminar for undergraduate students, on the topic "Women as Agents of Social Change." This would build on the rich history of the 19th century social reform movements, and proceed to explore the future possibilities with examples furnished by the women who took part in the Program.

Whether or not such new directions develop, the Suburban Training Program remains a worthwhile endeavor. It has demonstrated that an urban university can be an effective agent of social change, by extending its growth-enabling function of education and training to suburban nonprofessional women.

REFERENCES AND BIBLIOGRAPHY

Barnett, H. G. *Innovation: The basis of cultural change.* New York: McGraw-Hill Book Co., 1953.

Bernard, J. *Women and the public interest.* Chicago: Aldine-Atherton Inc., 1971.

Committee on Education. *Report to the President's commission on the status of women,* October 1963.

Farber, S. M., and Wilson, R. H. L., (Eds.). *The potential of woman.* New York: McGraw-Hill Book Co., 1963.

Ginzberg, E., *et al. Educated American women: Life styles and self-portraits.* New York: Columbia University Press, 1966.

Kiesler, C. A. *The psychology of commitment.* New York: Academic Press, 1971.

Knowles, M. Preface to M. R. Levin and J. S. Slavet, *Continuing education: State programs for the 1970's.* Lexington, Mass.: D. C. Heath & Co., 1970.

Lavell, M., and Cahill, E. E. Effects of an urban studies program for suburban women. In preparation.

Lerner, D. The educated woman as opinion shaper. *J. A. A. U. W.,* May 1970, 55, 260–262.

Lewis, E. C. *Developing woman's potential.* Ames, Iowa: Iowa State University Press, 1968.

Meyer, A. E. Leadership responsibilities of American women. In B. B. Cassara, *American women: The changing image.* Boston: Beacon Press, 1962.

Mitchell, J. C. *Social networks in urban situations.* Manchester, England: Manchester University Press, 1969.

Myrdal, A., and Klein, V. *Women's two roles: Home and work.* London, England: Routledge and K. Paul, 1968.

Sanford, N. *Self and society.* New York: Atherton Press, 1967.

Seward, G. H., and Williamson, R. C. (Eds.). *Sex roles in changing society.* New York: Random House, 1970.

Shaffer, H. B. Voluntary action: People and programs. Editorial Research Reports, March 5, 1969.

Suelze, M. Women in labor. *Trans-action,* Nov.–Dec. 1970, 8, 50–58.

Woodhouse, C. G. Volunteer community work. In B. B. Cassara, *American women: The changing image.* Boston: Beacon Press, 1962.

6. Off-Campus Involvement Programs

JOHN R. COLEMAN
PAUL E. WEHR

Part of today's uneasiness in the groves of academe comes about because of uncertainties about how to fuse the campus learning experience with off-campus experiences. Only in a few places is there any firm denial that the off-campus work can be educational in value. More often, there is an admission, perhaps a grudging one, that such work has educational worth but that its promotion, supervision, and valuation are scarcely the proper functions of a college.

There are good reasons for such doubts and cautions in the academic world. A sizable catalog of failures in off-campus programs, particularly in the urban areas, could probably be compiled. That catalog would document for all the skeptics the cases of poor planning, poor follow-up, poor relations with the urban area, poor evaluation, and poor politics back on the campus.

Yet the record is far from one-sided. There are some modest but important examples of successful programs that made an off-campus semester or year into an integral part of undergraduate education. In this paper, we cite the experience of Haverford College in one such program. It is far from perfect; it has had moments of deep pain and of doubt; it has not always been easy to sell either on campus or in the neighborhoods where our students work and study. Yet we believe, immodestly, that it has been a program of exceptional worth and that what we have learned from it will have impact elsewhere.

Before we describe the program and cite what we think we have learned from its first years, some general prejudices of ours need airing.

First, we make no case for all-classroom education, or all-off-campus education. Our case is for *both.* The wholesale attacks on campus education that come from some quarters these days strike us as silly at best. It is never necessary that all which is taught in class be directly relevant to a problem of the moment—but it is always necessary that there be some purpose to the teaching. Today's student cries of "irrelevance" seem directed more at ill-planned, unexamined courses in whatever the subject field than at those courses where the morning's headlines get short shrift. We defend classroom teaching whenever the teacher is inspired by his material, can communicate why that material matters, and will excite his students to use that material in disciplined ways.

But, equally, we defend off-campus education. It is not necessary that such experiences be wasteful, disjointed, and ultimately frustrating. It will be that bad for most students if the faculty simply pushes them off campus and says "learn what you can." But nothing in our experience tells us that the faculty's role is one bit less important in making the most of an urban involvement experience than it is in making the most of the campus hours. That role is different, and more humbling perhaps, but it remains critical.

Second, we believe such experiences can be evaluated just about as well as on-campus work is evaluated. (How much that says will depend on who hears it said.) All that happens in a classroom and that contributes to the growth of the student cannot be measured with any precision at all. A man or woman emerges from four years of undergraduate schooling, and we know that the final product is much more, in maturity, analytical skill, and emotional control, than the sum of all the carefully graded performances in his or her courses. We don't on that account avoid measuring such parts of progress as we can, and we don't assume that the whole job is done once we turn in grade sheets. So, too, with the off-campus semester. There are intelligent, effective questions that can be asked to measure some parts of what happened as a result of, say, involvement in the center city. Some other parts of the impact remain hazier; those latter parts offer no excuse for failing to measure what we can and for failing to ask hard questions about the true educational worth of such involvement. We are educators. Our job is not to set aside what we know about discipline and standards when we enter an urban affairs program; instead, it is to use whatever we have learned in a new, more confusing, and more challenging environment.

Third, we assume it is much too late in America's social history for us to tolerate pushing our students into the urban area as a laboratory from whose occupants they are to draw their data. The ghetto residents, in particular, have been through that bit enough by now. Effective involvement programs from now on are likely to be restricted to ones with two-way benefits, each side both giving and receiving. The key word is "involvement."

With these few biases aired, let us look more closely at what one small college is learning from its experiences in helping its students and those from other similar colleges to work and study in the urban areas of Philadelphia.

HAVERFORD'S EDUCATIONAL INVOLVEMENT PROGRAM

Precisely how an academic institution works out its responsibility to its students and metropolitan environment depends on its own unique conditions—size, governance, resources, and the like. Haverford's response has been largely through its Educational Involvement Program (EIP), a project of its Center for Nonviolent Conflict Resolution.

The EIP includes an urban semester, where students live in two Philadelphia neighborhoods and participate in one of three units, each of which has a particular field-work focus: urban education, community organization, and total-care institutions. Along with working in carefully supervised positions, students participate in a semester-long seminar specifically designed for reflection on the type of field work they do, and taught by a faculty person with special expertise in that area. *Topics in Urban Education,* for example, exposes teaching assistants to small group dynamics, innovative teaching techniques, and the broader problems of Philadelphia public education and race relations, and fosters a deep sense of group identification and mutual-support and comradeship which are especially useful for beginning teachers. For the total experience students receive a semester's credit.

When they return to campus, an effort is made to involve them in programs for change within the more affluent suburban and urban populations. With a more profound knowledge of the urban scene and its problems, and a deeper commitment to working for creative change, many of these students are effective indeed in stimulating attitude changes and constructive programs either in middle-class communities or in working-class and poverty areas if they are minority students.

When these students graduate, EIP helps to place them in jobs or graduate study which will make use of their experience and interest in the change-oriented professions. These guidance and follow-up functions of such a program are essential.

In addition to producing better educated students more committed to social action, the program has led us to a number of conclusions which bear on the future of the university and its relating productively to metropolitan communities and to its own students.

Developing Relationships with Urban Neighborhoods

We have found it both sensible and valuable to develop mutually-beneficial and stable ties with a very limited number of small communities. Such longer-term relationships tend to be less exploitive, with more accountability developing at both ends.

Urban neighborhoods can no longer be "studied" or otherwise used, with little concern by the intervening agent for the felt needs and immediate gain of the local population. The social science research project has long been a form of "grants imperialism" as concerns low-income communities. The academic institution has profited through overhead costs and prestige, and the careers of individual researchers advanced, but rarely has the community involved benefited at all or even been made aware of the project results.

It is evident that mutual trust, sound problem-selection, and cooperative action and research develop only where relatively stable relationships are systematically worked at, with both the community and the academic institution committing itself to longer-term programs of study *and* action. Such relationships may seem more threatening initially to the academic partner but they are infinitely more productive and satisfying for all concerned.

Certainly the opportunity for making significant impact on the problems of a community increases greatly with stable relationships. The "neighborhood approach" breaks down urban problems into manageable, comprehensible units. This helps neighborhoods which need both limited problems to attack and some visible signs of progress toward their solution to encourage leadership and engage more community members in action. A year of field work in one project neighborhood enabled a black student in EIP to help the community establish a now-prospering food-buying cooperative. In the same neighborhood a group of white students, doing block-organizing over a period of a year, by its presence motivated a black youth group to assume that program and assert itself as a major leadership force in the community.

For the students too, working with continuity in certain neighborhoods is important, for it affords them a mix of macro- and micro-views of urban problems. Viewed solely at the macro-level, such problems defy analysis. By viewing them as they confront certain neighborhoods and specific families, however, students gain in a cognitive sense —they understand the problems by seeing them at close range and with limited dimensions. They gain affectively, too, for incremental progress toward problem-solving is more visible. As students join community people in tackling concrete problems with some success, the political despair so endemic among students decreases. Commitment to working for change, which then seems possible after all, is enhanced. For both host neighborhoods and student field-workers then, the long-term neighborhood/university partnership provides two essential ingredients of constructive change—a realistic assessment of the situation, and hope.

In addition to being long-standing and honest, the relationship must be profitable for all concerned. The academic institution must be viewed as one resource for problem-solving and while it hardly has the answers to a neighborhood's problems, it can offer a certain expertness applicable to those problems. The community, for its part, provides a valuable learning environment for both students and faculty. The partner-institution can also contribute to the educational development of a community by accepting more of its youth as students, through curricular reform in its public schools, and through adult education. Not the least important payoff is a pattern of healthy interpersonal relationships across class and racial lines—ties which in Haverford's case have been exceedingly valuable.

Working with urban neighborhoods undoubtedly has its risks. Community politics threaten to involve even the most careful outside agent. With tact, sensitivity, and luck, however, the institution can minimize political involvement except in cases where physical expansion or other policies have direct impact on the partner-community. The risks are hardly a valid excuse for not becoming involved.

THE MIXED LEARNING EXPERIENCE

The value of experiential learning for a college's academic programs is great. Particularly in the social sciences, a mix of abstract reasoning and coursework, and direct experience with social systems and problems is essential for preparing students to lead relevant and healthy lives. The recent Ford (Ford Foundation, 1971) and Carnegie (The Carnegie Commission on Higher Education, 1971) reports on higher education come down especially hard on the side of reform through mixed learning.

> For many students, simply sitting in class and consuming the words and wisdom which college faculties produce is not a productive format for learning. ... many students learn best through involvement in concrete situations and practical tasks. This does not mean that such students are vocationally-oriented—some are, some are not. It means that their preferred medium for learning is not an abstract issue but a concrete problem, and the knowledge to be gained is subjective as well as objective. Information is absorbed and understood in terms of its relation to their overall task. (Ford Foundation *Report on Higher Education,* 1971).

Our own experience suggests something of the nature of mixed learning and why it is so rich for students exposed to it. The signs of their intellectual and emotional growth are striking. Most dramatic, perhaps, is the *autonomy* students develop in these projects. Their participation reflects a heady combination of self-knowing, self-testing, and self-reliance which produces psychologically mature persons as well as autonomous learning agents. As three of our students characterized it:

> (The experience) made me question my self-image and . . . the basis of many other ideas I held. Why was the way I saw things so different from the way certain other people saw those same things?

> This was a question with which I had not been forcefully confronted before. I had to face it in order to do my job, which involved working with people who might hold different basic viewpoints. I was led to look for the determinants of my values and those of other people.

> [The experience] was very enriching for me. I read a great deal on my own, learned how to observe what I saw around me and fit it into what I was learning in books. A sort of self-education thing. In general, I did more work reading and studying [there] in the academic sense than I ever did elsewhere.

> One . . . becomes more aware of one's surrounding and learns to automatically observe and describe the immediate situation—which is the first step to evaluative criticism.

Some will argue that facilitating such growth is not the function of a higher educational institution. We disagree. For four very formative years the college or university is the major facilitator or inhibitor of both a student's intellectual and emotional growth. We maintain that these do and must occur in concert and that the promotion of a harmony between the intellectual and the emotional should be of highest concern to an institution of higher learning.

The development of self-awareness and autonomy is important as well for the community with which students work, for they are basic to its ability to act productively in its own interests.

The development of autonomy in students is closely related to a *sense of empowerment* that they gain from their field work. The challenge, the immediate feedback, their successes and failures are all part of the highly educative process of interacting with one's environment. While Piaget applies his theories of action/environment interaction to children, the learning potential of such interaction would seem to operate at any level of learning, including science, where experimentation with and action upon a specific environment is a key to understanding it. By permitting the student to be an active rather than a passive learner of social science, off-campus education empowers him to grow in understanding both his socio-political environment and himself.

The structured and well-guided off-campus experience also facilitates for the student the *integration* of diverse and confusing stimuli into something approximating a coherent world-view. Higher learning, like all educational experience, should be an integrating process for the student, helping him to make sense of his world and to move toward creative techniques for changing some part of it. Campus and off-campus education alike have parts to play in that process.

This process of integration inevitably involves an initial period of disorientation and dissonance for the student, for there is no comfortable way to step from classroom to social action in an unfamiliar neighborhood. But such is a precondition of new learning. Nor is the discomfort short-lived. Many a student is able to analyze and articulate what has happened to him only after he has re-entered campus life, and perhaps only after he has entered his final year of college. By then things begin to fall into place for him, if they are ever going to do so, and the off-campus semester has then served as a catalyst for synthesizing his coursework and the world of action.

A student's knowledge of the urban scene and, in particular, how its institutions and communities operate, can be greatly enhanced through an inner-city semester. There is an opportunity to develop a healthy critical faculty for reading social science literature dealing with urban problems. This knowledge may be matched by a renewed interest in using the college's resources to explore issues and solve problems which experience has made real for the students. Interest would seem to improve performance too; at Haverford three-quarters of the students for whom adequate data are now available significantly raised their academic grades after the off-campus project.

There may be still other positive changes as a result of off-campus education. We believe we have seen a refinement of some students' empathizing skills, a refinement important both for personal mental health and for public attitudes supportive of constructive social change. Empathy crossing racial and class lines is especially important.

The off-campus semester may also reinforce certain positive values in students. Participating students probably have an above-average commitment to urban concerns to begin with; that is what brought many of them into EIP. However, with new information by way of both guided and unguided exposure to the full weight of the urban area's discrimination, exploitation, and even differences, the resolve to make a positive commitment to change deepens.

EVALUATION

In our experience, such off-campus education has significant payoffs. Whether it will be considered essential and adopted by colleges and universities in the future will depend partly on the skill and precision with which it is evaluated and its results presented to the academic community.

Some indicators of the educational worth of off-campus programs would include measurable differences in performance of control (nonparticipating) and experimental (participating) groups of students. A comparison of academic performance before and after participation is one possible indicator, and the degree of commitment to change as measured by a student's voluntary involvement in action programs is a second. Attitude shifts among participating students in such areas as racial feelings, self-perception, interpersonal skills, and commitment to working for change are measurable, in rough ways at least, by questionnaires administered before and after involvement. It is, of course, risky to attribute changes directly to participation because of the large number of uncontrolled variables. So, in the last analysis one must rely heavily on personal assessments by students of the impact of the experience on their behavior.

Of special interest to us at Haverford will be the long-range effects of off-campus education. Toward what areas of graduate study will the participants move? What occupational areas will attract them, what positions will they obtain, and how will their off-campus experience have affected all of this? Follow-up data are essential here; our work is far from done.

Finally, some sound study of the impact of such programs on host communities should be done. Has it been predominantly positive or negative, according to both objective and subjective criteria? Here input from the community is perhaps most vital.

INSTITUTIONAL RESISTANCE

Even with the most precise evaluation scheme and sensitive political actions, resistance to innovative programs is inevitable if only because change is generally resisted in any established organization. Off-campus education implies a new responsibility role for the institution vis-a-vis its students and its metropolitan milieu—one that rests on a holistic concept of higher education. For one thing, off-campus education calls for experimentation with new teaching methods which rely somewhat less on the established literature and traditional pedagogy, and somewhat more on group learning techniques. An on-site seminar, for example, can hardly be run as it would be in many a campus classroom. The needs of the students are quite different. Seminars need to be disciplined and reflective, but relaxed and flexible, and they require an unorthodox learning relationship—more communal and less teacher/student in nature. While a faculty member in such a setting is no longer on his "home turf," and may need exposure to concrete problems as much as his students, he does have a set of analytical skills and a knowledge of the literature which afford him *primus inter pares* status. Some teachers operate naturally more as facilitators of learning than as dispensers of knowledge, even in the regular curriculum, and their adjustment to the new relationship would be slight. For others, teaching effectively in such programs would require drastic modification in their teaching styles.

Whether an off-campus curriculum can be successfully grafted onto the institution's regular program will be determined by how successfully the threat of change can be redefined, for the faculty, as an asset. The need is to identify the change with the teacher's search for improvement in his teaching effectiveness, his research capabilities, and his personal commitment to using research skills directly in the interest of a more healthy and just society.

If a sizable number of faculty can be convinced of the value of off-campus education, they in turn will engage the imagination and participation of their students. Contemporary myth has it that the process operates in the reverse manner. We have found, though, that student demands for "relevance" in the curriculum may be symptoms of real dissatisfaction, but they do not lead students automatically to try constructive alternatives to what they decry. Most students need encouragement and even pressure from faculty and administration to move beyond the familiar. The campus remains a relatively secure and known world for students; while many of them may call what goes on there unchallenging or irrelevant, at least they know how to survive and sometimes be comfortable there. Alas! The greatest obstacle to development of off-campus education may once again be the problem of financial resources. Hard times on campus are not likely to be hospitable times for new programs. Time and competent people are needed to develop ties with communities, challenging and productive field-work positions, custom-fitted seminars, and other essential ingredients. Some one person must be responsible for program development. This can be a faculty member released for that purpose but he must have unusual interpersonal skills. It is hardly a task for a part-time committee, although such a group is indispensable for planning and advisory functions.

The truth remains that a serious effort in off-campus education cannot be made without some financial investment by the institution. In the economics of education as elsewhere, commitment and priorities are reflected in budget-line items. The likelihood of shifts in resource allocation will vary with the institution of course. The most successful if not the most permanent means of gaining institutional acceptance of new programs is to attract funds from private and government granting agencies. Sound innovation remains at a premium in higher education and an imaginative proposal containing a proper evaluation design continues to have a fair chance of being funded. That may be the best that can be said, until the day comes when our institutions of higher education put so high a premium on off-campus learning as a supplement to on-campus learning that they too re-order some priorities. The challenge is still out there, waiting.

REFERENCES

The Carnegie Commission on Higher Education. *Less time, more options: Education beyond the high school,* 1971.

The Ford Foundation. *Report on higher education,* April 1971.

7. Temple University and the Community Development Evolution

HERMAN NIEBUHR

INTRODUCTION

Temple University was founded in 1884 by Rev. Russell H. Conwell, author and deliverer of the famous "Acres of Diamonds" speech, as an institution to provide low-cost higher education for deserving and able Philadelphians of limited means. Temple, like many other urban colleges founded in the same era, was a typically American invention, much like the land-grant colleges, linking the upwardly mobile aspirations of immigrant and post-immigrant generations to the changing manpower requirements of an increasingly complex urban economy. Through its proliferating day and evening programs in 15 schools and colleges it has awarded over 100,000 degrees.

Since the end of the Second World War, the institution has moved through a period of extremely rapid growth, from an enrollment of 10,000 registered students in 1947 to the 40,000 of today. In order to hold down tuition it has moved from private status to becoming one of Pennsylvania's three state-related institutions. It has moved from an essentially undergraduate to an increasingly graduate focus. From a strip of houses and buildings along Broad

Street, the city's major north-south street, it has become a campus of 70 acres. More recently, as it has felt the multiple pressures of the nation's urban crisis, it has sought to accommodate to these pressures and move from the rhetoric of the "urban university" to its implementation. Finally, located in the center of Philadelphia's largest black community, and facing the demands stemming from the rise in aspirations of its neighbors, the University has sought to develop a new dimension of neighborliness.

The thrust of this paper is to review in more specific terms the issues within the evolutionary process sketched above and cull some of the lessons for community psychologists. The author, originally a clinical psychologist, has participated in this process since arriving at Temple University in 1957.

THE COMMUNITY DEVELOPMENT EVOLUTION

Viewed from the perspective of 1971, the decade of the Sixties was a period of substantial social policy innovation and flawed implementation of those policies. Also flawed was the understanding of psychologists and other human service workers of this policy evolution; only now is the field beginning to understand its implications.

To look back for a moment: during the late Forties and for most of the Fifties, the mental health and other human service professions were preoccupied with legitimizing themselves, upgrading training, establishing standards, and developing professional *Lebensraum.* Several embedded social policy assumptions guided this development. First, with the emphasis on therapeutic-remedial services for "ill, disturbed, maladjusted, and neurotic" clients, there was unspoken acceptance of the developmental adequacy of the larger social system. Certainly, these same professions gave little attention to prevention and development strategies. The policy shift to such strategies through the vast array of social legislation of the Sixties was, and certainly still is, dramatic in concept if not in delivery. Second, the mental health professions, and indeed all other professions, tended to live and work in semi-isolated service sectors, having little interchange with other fields and disciplines. Beginning with concern over "multi-problem" families in the late Fifties, and the professional traffic management problems they created, a growing awareness of interrelatedness of problems and services developed. The prevention and development strategies helped to accelerate the move from fragmentation to at least the idea of "wholeness." The Ford Foundation Gray Areas Program in 1959, the President's Committee on Juvenile Delinquency and Youth Crime in 1961, the War on Poverty in 1964, and the Model Cities Program in 1967 are exuberant examples of this new approach which seeks to aggregate the myriad of informal and formal social components into a better developmental and supportive environment.

As many critics have pointed out (see, for example, Moynihan, 1969; Marris and Rein, 1967; Piven and Cloward, 1971) these strategies were flawed by conceptual naivete and inadequacy of implementation. Clearly, there has been a retreat from a total systems-oriented comprehensive community development approach to a subsystems approach via education, welfare reform, manpower, housing, and health programs. The community mental health program is a particular "sleeper" in its *sotto voce* approach to prevention without clarifying the immense implications of the move. There is also a fair amount of breast-beating within the professions, a clear advance from the complacency of the Fifties, but still no profession has suggested that it resign *sine die,* or move to a higher level of public service by merging with any other. Similarly, institutions have undergone substantial change during the decade. Be it urban school system, city hospital, state employment service, or any other major urban service delivery agency, there is modification of scope and role, there is increased linkage to other institutions, and

there is also the restiveness characteristic of the professions. However, they are still intact, still supported by the
essentially same social mandate, and still more self-ori-
ented than client-oriented.

Nonetheless, viewed from the perspective of social policy advance, the community development evolution
comes close to being discontinuous from what went before, and generates the same social change ripples as did
the Income Tax Amendment, the right to collective bargaining, and the Social Security Act. In pragmatic American fashion, it is another instance of a "partial revolution."

THE TEMPLE UNIVERSITY RESPONSE: 1960–70

From the late Fifties on, pressures for change were
evident and responses began to appear. A group of action-
researchers at the School of Medicine's Department of
Psychiatry began to work at converting the local House of
Correction into more of a rehabilitation center, then
moved into a community development approach to the
renewal of the Skid Row area with the long-range objective of preventing a new Skid Row in Philadelphia (Blumberg, *et al.*, 1966) and then began a developmental
project aimed at improving psychotherapy for lower
socio-economic patients. Another group of faculty from
all divisions of the University created the Temple Metropolitan Area Study Committee to begin a program of in-
terrelated research and demonstration projects on urban
problems. Faculty became interested in improving the
campus development process and ensuring greater equity for displaced community residents. All of these activities and others of similar orientation were spontaneous;
they arose in the absence of any policy or managerial
encouragement.

In 1961 the blandishments of the Ford Foundation as
well as local encouragement led the University to support
the efforts of a small group of faculty to prepare a prospec-

tus for the first generation of comprehensive community development programs. The endorsement by the Foundation and later the Federal Government led to the organization and attempted implementation of that first generation effort. A variety of factors prevented its success, but the commitment of the institution at the highest levels remained constant in spite of controversy and dispute. Meanwhile, the social policy messages were getting through, and changes began to appear within the schools and colleges. A new Dean in the College of Education began to lead his faculty o a commitment to inner-city education that has yet to run its course. A Center for Community Studies was created with the double task of promoting interdisciplinary research and actively relating to neighborhood and urban problems. As the decade wore on, every school and college added new programs geared to the urban and neighborhood challenge.

Despite the positive responses of the educational establishment, heavily stimulated and supported by Federal grants, the University's campus development process continued to generate increasing community tensions and in time became a focus of community organization efforts which sought to induce a new sense of neighborliness in the institution. Despite its positive efforts, Conwell's institution, founded to serve the poor, was pictured as the "have" establishment by its "have-not" neighbors. From another perspective, the "success" of higher education in expanding and securing ample funds for its own buildings contrasted sharply with the essential failure of low-income housing programs. The contrast was clearly visible, and the raw inequity was not lost on Temple's neighbors.

By the middle of the decade, the fact of urban crisis was prominent in the institutional consciousness. Top leadership saw opportunity in the crisis and began to assert and embellish the idea of an "urban university," restating Conwell's commitment in the modern context and recalling the incomplete development of the land-grant idea.

At the same time another inquiry began: how does one organize an "urban university?" Does one maintain the separateness of the mainstream schools and colleges from the lower-status extension organization? Or does one seek to integrate the emerging problem-solving and invention tasks of the urban university into the existing research and degree-oriented schools and colleges? This issue is still far from settled at Temple or any other urban college and university. Yet, its resolution will in many ways determine the viability of the urban university for the rest of the century.

At this point, another urban pressure passed the threshold. Just when Temple and other aspiring institutions were beginning to raise admission standards and savor the prospect of the "good" students hitherto lost to the first-rank institutions, the pressure of the minorities for consideration in the light of their developmental disadvantage led to the first of what are now seven special programs for the admission and support of disadvantaged students. Approximately 10 percent of Temple's full-time day students now come from such programs.

The period from 1967–70 was especially difficult at Temple, as elsewhere, as the pressures grew and accommodations took place in an atmosphere of crisis and crisis management. Increasing pressures from the neighboring black community led to major adjustments in the campus development process and resulted in a commitment to increased neighborliness and a return to the community of twelve acres slated for university development. These agreements were summarized and legitimized in the Community-Temple Agreement of 1970, signed not only by community leaders and Temple officials, but also by the Governor of Pennsylvania, the Mayor of Philadelphia, and other public officials.[1] The special programs for the

---

[1] The agreement states that Temple University will keep all appropriate community groups informed concerning future projects for capital improvements within its Institutional Development District. Moreover, community groups are to participate in the planning process preceding capital improvement decisions.

disadvantaged continued to expand. Almost every school and college increased its relatedness to the community institution or delivery system with which it was ultimately concerned (e.g., College of Education and the public schools). The general student turmoil modified governance patterns and produced a variety of curricular innovations that moved toward "relevance." Several new colleges, particularly concerned with urban problems, were created: a School of Allied Health Sciences, a School of Social Administration, and a School of Engineering Technology. Moving toward the integrative model of university organization, the administration created a new Office of Urban Affairs as a staff and planning unit. In the aggregate, this period of intense disruption and crisis correlated with a rise in the institution's urban effort to the $ 11 million level of funding as shown by a recent survey.[2]

CENTRAL ISSUES OF THE SEVENTIES

In the past few years, there has been a noticeable decline of pressures from community, students, and institutions. There is understandable fatigue on the part of administrators. One senses both withdrawal and cynicism in the community and student constituencies as the hope inspired by excessive rhetoric evaporates. A mood of defensiveness is evident in the faculty move toward unionization. The negative national attitude toward higher education and public support of its activities is in marked contrast to the earlier days of a veritable blank check. It is a time for assessment and a revised agenda. Four pressing issues demand attention from social scientists.

1. *Social policy and social invention.* If the social policy advances of the Sixties were real, why did implementation fall so short? For a time there were ample

[2]The "Urban Projects, Temple University, 1970–71" survey conducted by the Office of Urban Affairs.

funds, commitment, and personnel eager to try new approaches. It can be argued that adequate attention was never given to the tough process of translating social policy into programs, into organizational imperatives, into staff competence via pre-service and in-service training, into client participation competence, and then via a feedback loop into modification for greater effectiveness. Social invention never got very far past the policy stage, and here the intellectual community must bear some responsibility.

The "wholeness" and interrelatedness aspects of the social policy thrust came at a time when the fragmentation and differentiation of knowledge via the staffed organization of the sciences was still pervasive. Hence, the very bureaucratic character of a university makes it inordinately difficult to consider approaches to the prevention-development strategy. Moreover, the rising support of and commitment to nonapplied research in the preceding quarter-century left problem-solving and social-invention tasks declassé and unrewarded.

One can look back at the College of Agriculture at the turn of the century and find a unique system which linked social concern with a basic research process, then to a technology development and social invention component, then to a dissemination process via the extension agent, and which finally through him provided critical feedback leading to new concerns, priorities, and refinements. The failure to generalize this unique American invention to the rest of the university and indeed its defeat by the German research model must be regarded as a tragedy of the twentieth century. Lewis Mumford (1971) comments on this problem in a much broader historical context.

The social sciences are particularly culpable. Psychology, during its rapid evolution during the first half of the century, has indeed been concerned with human change. This is true of both basic and applied psychology. There are psychologies of development, learning, motivation, and social process, and clinical and other applied psychologists spend their lives promoting behavioral change. Yet, the unawareness of embedded assumptions, the slow response to the community development evolution, and the pervasive failure of the field to act upon its unique knowledge and competence in the reform and revitalization of the university is a sign that bureaucratic concerns too often dominate the professional and scientific imperatives. Suffice it to say, a change-oriented society will demand that its intellectuals pay their dues in the rationalization of change. Adoption of the social invention role as manifest in the College of Agriculture model is still possible.

2. *Redesign of the service delivery systems.*   One of the major social invention tasks is the redesign of society's service delivery system. We have more of the rhetoric than the substance of redesign thus far. The add-ons of the past decade in education, health, manpower, and housing institutions which were partial accommodations to the community development evolution have created jerry-built structures in each of these institutions which make dubious sense and are difficult to manage. The field of education is an example. Coming out of the cognitive and character development ethos of the nineteenth century, education had profited from Freud and Dewey sufficiently to move the postwar generation into the middle class. However, the technological revolution, the concurrent movement of the present underclass minorities, and the present media-oriented generation of affluent humanists have raised the most serious question of education's vitality in a century. Such accommodations as early childhood programs in a human development framework and the introduction of paraprofessionals as cultural bridgers for the minorities may be symptoms of the more fundamental reform envisioned by Ivan Illich (1971). Clearly, there exists a need for advanced monitoring systems measuring the goodness of fit between the emerging genera-

tion and the existing development system, and psychologists ought to take the lead in inventing them.

Unhappily, the narrow parochialism of present graduate and professional education with its clear dominance of discipline over problem-orientation inhibits the psychologist from delving into the complexities of the major delivery systems in collaboration with others.

3. *Value evolution and the quality of life.* Prominent in the community development strategy is an evolutionary advance in societal values. Greater equity, opportunity, and humanity are the emerging values of the black community, young people, those interested in ecology, peace, sexual equality, population control, and preservation of natural resources. Psychologists, especially clinical psychologists and now community psychologists, are "value-carriers"; the first-half of the present century can be viewed as an epoch of emergent psychological freedom with its emphasis on individualistic humanism. Analysts, psychotherapists, counselors, and caseworkers were the acolytes and Freud was St. Paul. This psychological freedom was also part of the civilized revolt against the irrational authority of tradition, especially of the authoritarian religions. In its focus on individualism, it left untouched the larger issues of the social system, the family, the neighborhood, the economy, nationalism. Bronfenbrenner (1970) has recently suggested that the delicate balance between individuality and community may be becoming undone. Many of the phenomena of the youth culture suggest a groping for community identity and satisfactions. Must not psychologists address themselves to this problem?

The domination of the research ethic over the past quarter-century has made it unfashionable to discuss the value issues as openly as they need to be discussed. The value dilemmas of American society, especially of the emerging generations and the minorities, find the academic community still fixated at another level of value development. It may well be that this gap has had more to do with the rapid decline of academic prestige and status than any other single factor.

4. *Clinical psychology and community mental health.* As psychology's contribution to the therapeutic-remedial phase of the mental health movement, clinical psychology played a useful role in introducing critical evaluation of earlier therapeutic dogmas and helping move behavioral change technology from the dominant medical ethos. But it too became trapped in the therapeutic-remedial context and played no role in the emergence of community development strategy. Community mental health clearly attacked the social class bias of earlier therapeutic approaches and tentatively stepped into the community development area through the consultative-community education-community organization door. However, as the earlier comprehensive community development projects showed, unless professionals are radically retrained, either by their own inclination or by design, they tend to use the same thought and action systems they used in earlier professional settings. It has been the author's observation that community mental health programs are largely unaware of the realities of neighborhood organization and the operation of the other service delivery systems which "intend" to improve education, employment, recreation, and housing among other critical services. Yet, it is precisely these services in interaction with individual clients and the larger community that contribute to the developmental-supportive environment. To affect it in an advocacy and planning sense requires specific knowledge of these subsystems, their embedded values, and points of intervention. If this analysis is correct, and if it were implemented, it is likely that community mental health would not long have the political viability to continue that role. The dilemma is consid-

erable: to remain naive will tend to ensure survival, but to grow knowledgeable risks it.

The point is really that psychologists, like other human service personnel, need to move beyond the narrow conceptual and service contexts to which training has restricted them and begin to locate themselves within the "wholeness" of the community development context, as a means of providing better service and surviving the political struggles yet to come.

THE ROLE OF THE UNIVERSITY

The central theme of this paper, illustrated by the odyssey of Temple University in the past decade, is that the concept of "wholeness" in intellectual thought and social policy is discontinuous with the fragmentation of thought and policy in preceding decades, and that the therapeutic-remedial institutions and professions which came to life in the first half of the century must now accommodate to a prevention-development strategy that is still in the early stages of implementation. Each of the major institutions and service delivery systems is undergoing painful and grinding changes as it moves to accommodate, usually without understanding the breadth of this cultural trend. The university is a critical institution in this drama. Two among the various ways in which it can contribute to community development will be mentioned here.

The conversion of professions and institutions into service delivery systems requires a new concept of personnel classification, training, and upgrading. Yet, the university's professional curricula are still based on turn-of-the-century assumptions of professional practice. While this is partly a function of a dogged resistance to change, there has yet to be invented the service delivery concepts, organizational structures, and processes that can link professional, paraprofessional, and client in a more dynamic system. As the manpower developer and credentialer of the most highly trained personnel, does not the university have an obligation to direct its critical, analytic, and creative competence to these tasks?

Although research is usually one of the two or three key elements in the definition of a university, it can be argued that an analysis of both societal need and the reality of institutional behavior make it too narrow. The imperatives of a change-oriented society, especially in this period of community development policy evolution, require not only adequate knowledge but also a mechanism to relate that knowledge to social needs through problem-solving, invention, technological development, dissemination, and a critical feedback loop. Despite the rhetoric of the research ethic, many of these activities go on, not legitimized like the College of Agriculture model and very often without reward, but they do exist and seem to be growing. It has been suggested that research and the rest of the related activities come under the rubric of innovation, and that innovation and the socialization function become the definition of a university.

CONCLUSION

This paper has attempted to describe how one institution, Temple University, located in the heart of a large city, and more specifically in the largest black neighborhood of the city, has sought to cope with the urban crisis and policy innovations of the Sixties. As the discussion of those accommodations and ensuing problems reveals, the University is only at the end of the beginning. The acceleration and rationalization of the change-process is most difficult in what is, after all, a consensus-based institution. As its next step in this direction, Temple University is presently organizing a new planning structure and process. Hopefully, it will focus faculty, student, and staff competence on these and other pressing issues. By uncovering its own embedded assumptions and irrationalities, and relating itself to the larger cultural trends, it will continue to renew itself. Since the institution's proper focus is on man, the role of psychologists, research and applied, is clear. They must be concerned with social invention and implementation, with monitoring and feedback systems, with value dilemmas, and with the community as a whole. The emergence of community psychology is a welcome expansion in both the moral and the scientific and professional vision of the field.

REFERENCES

Blumberg, L., Shipley, T., and Niebuhr, H. The development, major goals and strategy of a skid row program. *Quarterly Journal of Studies of Alcohol,* June 1966. See also Diagnostic and Rehabilitation Center. Philadelphia's skid row project, a demonstration on human renewal. Interim Report, 1965. (304 Arch St., Philadelphia).

Bronfenbrenner, U. *Two worlds of childhood: U.S. and U.S.S.R.* New York: Russell Sage Foundation, 1970.

Illich, I. The alternative to schooling. *Saturday Review,* June 19, 1971.

Marris, P., and Rein, M. *Dilemmas of social reform: Poverty and community action in the United States.* New York: Atherton Press, 1967.

Moynihan, D. P. *Maximum feasible misunderstanding.* New York: Free Press, 1969.

Mumford, L. *The myth of the machine: The pentagon of power.* New York: Harcourt, Brace, Jovanovich, 1971.

Piven, F. F., and Cloward, R. A. *Regulating the poor: The functions of public welfare.* New York: Pantheon Books, 1971.

Part III

PSYCHOLOGISTS AT WORK IN OTHER COMMUNITIES

8. University Involvement in the Community

FRANK J. CORBETT
MURRAY LEVINE

PART I: HISTORY OF NEWEST UNIVERSITY-COMMUNITY PARTNERSHIP

The university's tradition of isolation from society sustains its image of the "ivory tower." With the exception of the involvement of some universities in Defense Department research and the private consulting activity of individuals, the university rarely accepted any direct responsibility for solving problems in its surrounding community. Some of its divisions, such as medical school hospitals, provided service to the community, but usually the teaching and research needs of the medical school dominated other considerations, sometimes to the detriment of community service (Duff and Hollingshead, 1968). Schools of education, social work schools, and graduate programs in psychology have for a long time placed students in community service facilities for the purpose of training; however the schools or programs were rarely offered the opportunity to become involved in changing the agencies in which their students were placed or the system of service delivery in which the students were

137

involved. Nor did the schools or programs accept any substantial responsibility for fostering such change.

In the early 1960's, concepts of community orientation and prevention in the field of mental health were beginning to make themselves felt as the Joint Commission on Mental Illness and Health made its recommendations to the Congress, to the President of the United States, and to the profession at large (Joint Commission, 1961). In related but broader areas, the Ford Foundation sponsored the Great Cities Program, attempting to examine intensively problems of urban blight, delinquency, and the delivery of services in the cities (Marris and Rein, 1967). These events brought about a level of university involvement in community affairs that exceeded past tradition.

By the mid-1960's a number of other important events combined to place new demands on universities to end their isolation from their surrounding communities. The Kennedy administration's emphasis on domestic involvement, which was continued by the Johnson administration's program for the Great Society, made available funding for projects designed to develop needed social change. Many academicians, particularly those in the human services fields, were given opportunities to contribute to the resolution of social problems which in the past had been neglected by the Federal government.

The new Federal-university fellowship was paralleled by the swift growth of involvement by university students and faculty in the issues of poverty and civil rights. This activity reached an explosive and emotional crest with the assassinations of the Kennedys, Martin Luther King, Jr., and Malcolm X. The campus saw the development of an active, vocal alliance of university students, dissident professors, and poor blacks demanding that the university assume a posture of relevance to the problems of poverty and racism. Universities either froze or precipitously mobilized scanty resources in an attempt to respond affirmatively to the demand. The actions evoked praise from some, criticism and resistance from others, and still more vigorous demands for greater university involvement in public affairs. Simultaneously, as the university formulated strategies for expanding its service to its surrounding community, ideologies of self-help and community control made an auspicious appearance.

University service took at least three different forms. First, some academic departments began to investigate new ways to relate to community agencies and groups. Second, universities established service centers, frequently designated as offices of urban affairs, which were relatively independent of the teaching and research responsibilities of a given department. Third, universities became concerned with recruiting minority students and faculty and providing curriculum, supporting services, and related facilities. What follows is an account based on personal experiences with programs of the first and second kinds.

PART II: THE UNIVERSITY DEPARTMENT

The university, like most institutions, has a system of values, the measures of which determine its success. One measure of success for the university is its national reputation, built largely upon the national image of the university's faculty. The same factors which contribute to national image universally play an influential role in the university's promotion policy. These are: (1) publishing, (2) research grants, (3) participation in national and international meetings, and (4) invitations to give colloquia at other universities. Of the four factors, university departments have traditionally placed great emphasis on publishing. Departments typically affix a great deal of pride to national standing, which is largely based on the publication of faculty research. The social organization of departments, especially as it is manifest in relatively light faculty teaching loads, grants a faculty member a great amount of freedom to use his time as he sees fit. The autonomy of the faculty member and his striving toward reputation and promotion foster feelings of competition among faculty, and reduce the drive toward cooperative activity. The tenure system in major universities serves as a natural selection device for strongly competitive individuals, and the social organization maintains their competitiveness. Teaching and research (particularly in graduate education), and not service delivery, are always paramount in the development of a department-based community service program. The values placed on publication, faculty autonomy, teaching, and research frequently constrain the potential efficacy of department-based community-oriented programs. A discussion of the advantages and disadvantages that arise from these values follows.

Publishing is a complex and delicate subject for the faculty member. Junior faculty are hired for their research potential, and are promoted or given tenure when that potential finds fruition in the form of a quantity of publications. Promotion to the status of full professor is most often based upon the publication of one or more books which are well received professionally. This aspect of how a published piece is received is most subtle, and often involves academic fashion and snobbery, although quality is a major consideration.

The dictates of academia have traditionally given more value to techno-scientific writings than to nonquantitative or popularly oriented works, even though the content of the latter may have significant social import. The values and traditions of a university, where those interested in applied work are in the minority, necessarily limit the amount of support for applied research. Academicians frequently do not recognize the real problems of doing research in the field setting. Thus, in one case, a colleague who developed a field project which is currently cited as a model for projects of its kind in guidelines for grants from a national agency was denied a prize in research competition because his work "lacked rigor." The prize-winning effort was a laboratory analogue of a counseling problem, considerably less exciting and significant, but much better designed. In another instance, a colleague was denied tenure despite his clinical and field research, which had major impact on the policies of an important governmental agency. In still another instance, a report of a five-year clinical field study, which in the opinion of several qualified scholars produced new knowledge of vast substance, was denigrated as "journalism" by a senior faculty person at a meeting in which the author's promotion was under consideration.

Publication outlets present still another problem. The value of a publication is weighted by which journal or press published it. When one is dealing with new content, the traditional prestigious journals may not find the materials suitable for their use, and the work may be considered less valuable because it was published in a less prestigious outlet.

The effects of promotion policies based on publication present constraints that extend beyond determining the success or failure of individual faculty career interests. If a faculty member chooses to follow his interests and is denied tenure, continuity of a service program will be disrupted.

At universities which emphasize graduate education, work is organized to facilitate research and scholarly output. The social organization of most departments permits a faculty member the freedom to use his time as he sees fit. No one on regular line appointments works for anyone else. Beyond the constraint imposed by the dictates of teaching loads, and some minimal constraints on the use of faculty time for outside, paid consultation, a faculty member may virtually do as he pleases. Chairmen have some power, but they usually cannot invade faculty time. Untenured faculty are in somewhat more vulnerable positions in terms of needing support among senior faculty, but tenured faculty are quite independent of each other.

Faculty can freely select their associations and activities. An influential leader may gather a group of coworkers, provide them with additional rewards in consultation fees, summer salaries, or research money, but he usually cannot compel involvement of either junior or senior faculty. There is often competition for the loyalty, interest, and affection of graduate students among faculty, leading faculty to develop their own following and teams. The freedom of faculty to do as they please and the competition among them are factors which limit the development of large scale, cohesive, community-oriented action programs from a departmental base.

While autonomy is a firmly held value, academicians are deeply suspicious of empire builders, because of the assumption that the empire is built through skill in faculty politics or grantsmanship, and not because of academically valued productivity. If a new program threatens to upset the balance of power within a department, or if there is conflict with other university-wide interests, a proposed program may be blocked. For example, the administration of a major university with a history of conflicted involvement in public education prevented a senior professor from accepting a sizable grant in teacher education. Veto power may be exercised over programs which threaten to absorb resources or which seem out of keeping with whatever is considered the primary business of the department. The problem is difficult enough in a time of expanding resources, but it is particularly acute for a developing program in a period of declining resources. Competition among specialties to fill faculty openings and the infighting for space, secretarial assistance, and graduate student support can be fierce.

Despite facile assertions to the contrary, departments value the teaching function, particularly in graduate education. Educational needs will predominate even when an academic department develops a service facility. Department-based psychological clinics tailor their case loads to the needs of practicum courses, or to research requirements. They could not do otherwise and justify the operation. Community-oriented service facilities also have to absorb students and provide for their education, but the students are placed in host facilities not under the control of the university department. The host facilities have their own needs, and these may not be fully congruent with the teaching needs of the department.

A few examples may illustrate the problem. A school consultation program was designed in part to provide for the training of graduate students. Many of the students did well, but a few created conflict with some teachers or a principal. The conflicts invariably led to problems in maintaining a working relationship with the setting. While such problems are expected, such conflict may jeopardize the relationship with the host setting permanently. As a second example, when one tries to provide for preclinical observational experience, the host settings agreeing to cooperate may find themselves overwhelmed with requests, beyond their capacity to absorb students. Moreover, when one program starts to make such arrangements, others quickly follow with the consequence that cooperative facilities tend to be inundated by offers of assistance.

Research needs present a special problem. After a relationship is established with a particular setting, the leadership and staff may agree to cooperate with a research request. However, continued requests can become a nuisance. When a faculty member develops access to "subjects," it is common for colleagues to ask to be permitted to use the facilities for their purposes. In a prison project, colleagues requested that students be permitted to use inmates for studies unrelated to the corrections mission. In schools, the relationship between the experimental design and research problem and immediate educational needs is often quite moot.

The research itself may be perfectly respectable, but such demands create a problem for the community-oriented program. On one hand, refusals to cooperate may cost valuable internal political support, and on the other, assistance to students and colleagues may cause people in the institutional setting to feel exploited, as they too often are.

A dilemma is presented when one attempts to develop research in order to fulfill the academic teaching mission. We would like to encourage students to take on research in field settings. However, field settings typically do not meet the requirements of research design, as these are taught in the graduate methods courses. Moreover, field studies are uncertain, and students have graduate education timetables to meet. If we encourage students to take on field problems they may find difficulty in applying the methods they have been taught, or in convincing non-field-oriented professors that the rigor of laboratory research is inappropriate to many field problems.

Publication, in terms of protecting the interests of the people within the field settings, presents still another issue of considerable consequence. Articles even mildly critical of the host setting may completely destroy any possibility of a continued relationship, and the academician is often insensitive to this point. His commitment to objectivity is not necessarily shared by those who earn their living in the setting he criticizes.

Despite these and other difficulties, we have found it possible to work out relationships with a variety of community agencies. From the university's end there are definite advantages. For faculty there is the advantage in terms of exciting work and, occasionally, of earning consulting fees. The relationships also provide for the faculty member an immediate personal experience that lends authenticity and credibility to teaching that is attainable in no other way. Working out a relationship with community agencies provides observational and field facilities for some students. On several occasions, we have had the pleasure of having students tell us that their field experience was easily the most exciting and profitable part of their entire educational career.

Agencies also benefit. Frequently there is free or low-cost service. We have provided a significant number of students for a lay counseling center. In the early days of its operation, a significant number of the "hot line" telephone volunteers at a crisis center came from our student body. A Model Cities program absorbed some graduate students and put their academic skills to good use in program writing. A community-based nursery school has made good use of student consultants, at no cost to the school. A penitentiary had the advantage of a variety of psychological services, at no cost, because a good training situation was provided. In many of these instances no other service of the kind mentioned would have been available without the university program.

The university provides a limited employment service for community agencies, with mutual benefits. Agencies needing services come to the university department requesting recommendations for filling vacant staff positions. We have been able to suggest students and others for given openings. These recommendations are important, especially to those agencies which have little contact with the professional mental health community.

Personnel in various agencies enjoy the contact with university people. Agency directors tell us that students keep their people alive by asking questions. They also relate experiences which tell us that our willingness to have students work with agency personnel is regarded as a sign of the merit of the agency and its services, thereby providing a boost in morale. Relationships with agency workers have resulted in contacts with people one would not ordinarily meet. In turn, these contacts have on occasion ripened into other program opportunities. Sometimes personal relationships have been helpful in obtaining interagency cooperation and in expediting referrals for service. Invitations by agency personnel to discuss their work in seminars with our students have proven very valuable as a means of getting to know people, and as a means of introducing our students to work they would not otherwise encounter. On several occasions such invitations to community agencies have resulted in cooperative opportunities for work with our students.

If we assess our own efforts and those of our colleagues who operate from a base in a university department, we can show that broader experiences are provided for students, and training in varied modes of intervention is offered. However, a coherent large-scale program with its own style and values is yet to be developed. Efforts at promoting change in other institutional settings have met with success which can be characterized either as minimal or at best modest. In many instances, goodwill of community groups toward the university has resulted, but in a few, conflicts with agencies have led to continued enmities.

In a few instances, programs such as Goldenberg's residential youth center (Goldenberg, 1970) and Bard's police family crisis intervention unit (Bard and Berkowitz, 1967) have had profound impact well beyond the project's initial demonstration intent. However, both projects were more offshoots rather than intimately related to psychology departments. In both instances, at points of crisis the respective psychology departments failed to provide adequate support. The success of the two programs and their impact occurred despite many of the characteristics of the departments, and only in part because of them. The scholarly output of these and programs like them is increasing and improving in quality.

We do not hesitate to assert that our own intellectual growth has been enhanced and our clinical and research interests changed as a consequence of our community involvement. However, the strong organization and cultural identity of the academic department has maintained itself, albeit with some small modification, against the demands of community-oriented work.

Part III: The Urban Affairs Office

As an alternative to seeking change in academic departments, university administrations have tended to answer the call to service by creating new offices specifically geared to providing services to the surrounding community. If that community happened to be poor and black, the office was frequently given the urban affairs designation. Offices of this kind were frequently created overnight, sometimes in response to some immediately available funding opportunity, but often with a tenuous foundation. The accusation that such offices were initially instituted as much for purposes of public relations as they were for providing real services is both cynical and debatable. That they were established with a minimum of forethought and knowledge about urban problems is not a debatable proposition at all, as subsequent events amply demonstrated.

The example with which we have some familiarity was an urban affairs office created with some fanfare outside of the regular academic departments, and initially funded in part by a federal grant. It was staffed by an interdisciplinary group with impressive academic credentials in fields appropriate for its mission. The director was an urban planner with an advanced degree from a leading university. Other members of the staff represented law, education, social science, and the health-related sciences.

Because of the circumstances that influenced its creation, the staff was fairly free to innovate and implement programs without being bound by the traditional constraints that regulate the operations and styles of established departments. The group was able to determine its own policies for the selection of staff and for fixing salaries. It determined its own procedures for developing programs, selecting target areas and modes of intervention, and for establishing its own standards of accountability. The group was given adequate office space, a generous budget, and a number of other extra resources it deemed necessary to expedite the organization of programs. Chief among these resources was a direct line to the two top administrators of the university. These features combined to give the program an enviable distinction and, in a sense, explain some of its early successes. However, the same features turned out to be a source of some of the difficulties which confronted the program later, difficulties similar to those other universities are encountering even today.

In its early years, the office performed services that not only satisfied some previously hostile community interests, but also served to assure the program's continuance after the pressures that influenced its creation had waned, and after support money had been substantially reduced. For example, it played a catalytic role in securing a Model Cities program for the community. It sponsored a television series that generated widespread public interest in a range of urban issues. It also played a prominent role in the early development of various special programs through which appreciable numbers of educationally and economically handicapped minority group students gained entrance into the university. The special programs were a strong force for ushering in a cordial relationship between the university and the black and Puerto Rican populations that had never before existed. Before the programs were established, the university had a very poor record for enrolling minority group students.

The urban affairs office won additional acceptance after it opened four storefront community service centers in the heart of the black ghetto areas. In addition to making needed educational and social services easily accessible to ghetto residents, the centers provided a vehicle that enabled black residents to exercise an unusual amount of administrative and policy control over the operation of the centers. For the university, the centers provided readily available stations that afforded faculty and students expanded opportunities to perform a variety of services in the community. For the urban affairs office, the storefront center projects provided a range of experiences which ultimately led the office to make a radical shift in the focus of its community services, nearly three years after the storefront project was initiated. The shift followed a serious self-appraisal by the office's personnel after the relationship between the project's community leadership and the office staff had significantly deteriorated. From the self-appraisal came the discovery that the urban affairs office's character had been shaped by the storefront center projects and, therefore, by the character and style of the communities the projects served. Another result of the self-appraisal was the fact that the office lacked a solid identity with the culture of the university, and had failed to develop a culture of its own. Consequently, the office was powerless to fight off domination by the projects.

Because the university's urban affairs office failed to define the scope of its mission and the limits of its service to the community, members of the target population defined them according to their own perspectives. Their perspectives differed sharply from those of the university, and the differences dominated the interactions for nearly two years. For example, militant spokesmen for the community viewed the projects as an instrument for accommodating the community's desire to exercise complete control over program planning and implementation, hiring and termination of the projects' staff, and fiscal matters. The spokesmen found support of their views in their interpretation of guidelines established by the state agency responsible for the administration of the Federal grant-in-aid legislation, which provided most of the funding support for the projects. The guidelines included a mandate that the client group participate in the planning and execution of programs. The mandate was defined with the same vagueness that has fostered widely varying interpretations of the resident participation concept since its introduction in the Economic Opportunity Act of 1964 (Moynihan, 1969; Cole, 1971). The director of the urban affairs office interpreted the guidelines to mean that the university's accountability for the Federal grant could not legally be delegated to the community group. Consequently, acquiescence to the community's desire was impossible.

These differences led to the surfacing of genuine distrust and bitter hostility toward the university. Militant community leaders of one storefront project made capital of the situation, sometimes for what appeared to be a selfish motive, namely, to further cement their leadership status and their influence over the management and direction of the program. Their chief tactic was to criticize the university with vitriolic denunciations, make intractable demands, and express an implacable desire for retribution. The leaders successfully stifled any opposition to their views by insisting that the university's involvement in the program was motivated by disguised paternalism, by underscoring specific instances in which the university had not kept what they considered to be firm promises, and by "bad mouthing" the program in the community. The needs of the people, unquestionably great, were usually expressed by these leaders in demands for services that exceeded those stipulated in the state's grant award.

The university found itself in the difficult position of "middle man" between the state funding agency and the inner-city project. As a result, the university had to assume the full responsibility for all unfavorable developments and, of course, the full brunt of the attacks, whether they were justified or not. The dilemma was intensified by contradictions in the state's eligibility guidelines. On the one hand, the guidelines mandated resident participation in all phases of the project's operations but, on the other hand, held the university unilaterally accountable for the administration of the grant. Further, the guidelines mandated a strong governance role for the people served by the program, but specified the program areas for which the grant was to be used.

These areas were often in conflict with the changing definition of the needs and desires of one center's resident Board of Directors. Resident participation was defined by the state funding agency in terms of shared responsibility between the university and the board. However, most of the board members emphatically rejected this definition; they insisted upon defining the concept in terms of complete control over the program and the funds as well. The university and its urban affairs office, powerless to delegate such control to the community group, understandably became the mau-maued flak catcher (Wolfe, 1971).

By this time, most of the original staff of the urban affairs office had either left the university or returned to the safe havens of their departments.

As the program of the storefront centers developed—and it did, despite the previously mentioned conflicts—the organizational weakness of the urban affairs office became more apparent. This weakness served to the advantage of the resident leaders. Having neither a culture nor a clearly defined mission of its own, the office had no resistance to the powerful pressures of community expectations and demands. Constantly on the defensive, the office was powerless to deal with the patronage system which one resident leader had cleverly instituted and controlled. At the same time, internecine rivalry dominated all deliberations of the resident board, with the result that program development and board opposition to the take-over by one individual were both stifled. Many of these problems would have been inconceivable in a program operated by any academic department, for a department would have been constrained to respond to demands in relation to its own values and structure.

Despite the conflicts, the mutual benefits of the inner-city project to the university and to the community also became more apparent. A plan had crystallized whereby the urban affairs office would make use of its ties to the university base in order to help assure the development of more effective programs at the largest storefront center. Two graduate social welfare students were engaged in a professionally supervised practicum to collect descriptive information about educational, employment, health, and welfare services that were readily available to troubled ghetto residents, and to compile the information into a directory. The completed directory was unique in that the 170 listings included 47 diverse, ghetto-based community action programs that were not included in any other directory. Moreover, the descriptions were simply written, and were cast in such a way that persons without a good formal education could efficiently use them.

While the directory fulfilled the primary purpose of providing a resource for a community-based, resident-manned counseling service, it also provided training for the social welfare students. Although there was cooperation with the storefront center's staff, the graduate students provided the important skills to develop a product of high quality. Actually the directory had a great sales value, having been so well put together that it was used by the center as a fund-raising tool. Here for the first time, a university-oriented mission of training entered the picture. Characteristics of the university culture emerged, and began to have some influence on the operation of the center.

The completion of a neighborhood problems-census project, jointly conducted by the center's staff and another graduate social welfare student, was also a part of a closely supervised practicum. The project resulted in the not surprising conclusion that stagnation and ineffectiveness were notable characteristics of service delivery in a ghetto area.

To deal with this problem the center's manager and the student undertook a low-key pilot project which had two aims: (1) to generate interest in coordination of services without arousing the mistrust and suspicion that already characterized the relations among agencies and institutions serving the area, and (2) to experiment with the development of a coordinating and communication vehicle that would be acceptable to both ghetto residents and the agencies and institutions.

At a previous point in time, the urban affairs office might well have become thoroughly entangled in the complex thicket of agencies and their conflicts. However, by emphasizing the teaching and training mission of the university, both the office and the community were spared the embarrassment of a fruitless encounter. The student made contact with various groups, and learned first hand about the issues and some of their effects on life in the community. At the same time, the effort did not place the office in the position of "middle man," nor did it hold out any ambiguous promise to deliver resources. The project also served to make some new friends for the university and to help some community groups, formerly strangers to each other, to know each other better.

A central aspect of university culture is the value it places on research, both for its own sake and as a means of developing information on which to base action. In recent times, as we have indicated, research has been viewed by community groups as exploitative. The very word can be an impediment in relationships with community groups. Nonetheless, when the university-based service preserves its own values, but adapts the form to the problem at hand, mutually beneficial results may be obtained.

In this context, a rewarding experience emerged from the office's involvement with an inner-city group, all black, that had been trying for nearly a year to organize an action program to deal with a condition that had caused much anguish in the neighborhood. As is so customary in economically depressed neighborhoods, the group's initial efforts centered around the preparation of a proposal for program funds. As is also customary, the problem and needs were defined on the basis of personal feelings and unsupported claims.

The university's urban affairs office entered the picture by happenstance. After four meetings with the group, a faculty representative of the office found substantial evidence that a pervasive sense of failure dominated the group's deliberations. The finding prompted the representative to offer the services of two student interns to help the group conduct a simple research project in order to provide factual bases for planning. The offer initially met with stern opposition. It was largely based, with some justification, upon conceptions that research, especially by university personnel, was self-serving and its only purpose was to look for and highlight the bad qualities of black people.

Opposition to the urban affairs office's offer of assistance relaxed after the faculty representative had assured the group that the project would be theirs and, significantly, after he had clearly delineated the nature and limits of the university's assistance. This was possible only because by this time the mission and structure of the office had been more clearly defined. Consequently, the faculty representative was able to explain with complete candor that attendant to the offer of assistance was the hope that the group would lend its knowledge, based upon its own research, to assist him with carrying out his obligation to train students for effective work in depressed ghetto areas at some later time. He also clearly outlined the kinds and volume of assistance the group could expect from the students and the services they could not be expected to perform. With the resident group's approval, the students, under close faculty supervision, began to apply the skills they had learned in the classroom, namely, to help the group to conduct its own research and to assist the group with developing a program that would reflect good planning. The group was helped to raise money so that it could hire indigenous residents to conduct interviews, analyze the results, with assistance, and to recommend a program, as well as a program structure, for the group's approval.

The whole project resulted in an abundance of goodwill. The community group had accomplished its mission of preparing a proposal that won for it funding support and the distinction of being the first inner-city group in the city to apply full-scale planning as a launching point for program development. For the university the goal of a student training mission was most satisfactorily fulfilled. Here it seems most appropriate to underscore that the group's satisfaction was manifest in one of the objectives of the program that finally emerged from the planning experience: a voluntary offer to cooperate with the university in conducting research that would be mutually beneficial to the neighborhood and the university.

Involvement of the urban affairs office with the storefront centers had an important value which had not been anticipated, and which enabled the office's white interns to continue to perform services in a ghetto area, despite the prevalent antiwhite attitudes there. Influential blacks mounted an effective movement, justifiable in a number of cases, which convinced many residents that the presence of white university people in the area was motivated only by a wish to obtain information that would enable them to write books and papers that "low rate" black people. In one instance the movement was defused by the manager of one storefront center after she had become convinced that the white students who worked at the center had several competencies which the center needed and, further that they had no other motive than to serve the center. Similarly convinced, the leader of another inner-city project in which interns of the urban affairs office were involved made it publicly known that he would "do battle" with anyone who tried to prevent his white volunteers from coming into the neighborhood.

These experiences led the urban affairs office to develop a preinterventive educational design for its student interns which had the following objectives: (1) to help them to identify one or more of their precise skills; (2) to adapt the skills to the needs and styles of their assigned neighborhood; and (3) to prepare the students for performance at the *how to* or implemental level of problem solving. Experience has taught us that both the university and the faculty "blow" their opportunities to render services and pursue their education in black ghettos by not convincing deeply troubled blacks that they have discrete skills to offer, that is, skills which are not available within a given neighborhood and which promise to contribute substantively to the pursuit of a neighborhood goal.

The lessons learned from these and other involvements in inner-city ghetto areas figured prominently in the restructuring of the urban affairs office. Three of these lessons are worthy of brief mention. First of all, failure of so many university ghetto-based programs is largely attributed to marked inattention to systematic planning. Consequently, ghetto residents, honestly believing they can solve their own problems, are encouraged to develop superficial programs. They invariably conceive the idea for a program, write a simple proposal, and, if funds are made available, initiate the program. Seldom are ghetto residents given the opportunity to conduct research, formulate definitive goals, test the workability of program forms and procedures, formalize a sound operational structure, hire and train staff, and perform other essential planning tasks. Seldom do university groups encourage and enable ghetto residents to plan their programs with the thoroughness that universities claim as one of their marks of distinction.

Second, university intervention in the complex and pernicious problems of ghetto areas indubitably will exacerbate the demoralization and bitter hostility already rife in these areas if any of the following conditions exist: (1) the interventive agent lacks an organization and culture that embodies clear values, goals, methods, and the appropriate administrative structure to operationalize the involvement; (2) the university agent lacks sufficient "free" money to finance the execution of a program or to back up a commitment; (3) the intervenors lack adequate knowledge of the sociology of the target area, its relations to the larger community, and the varying life styles of the inhabitants; (4) intervention is motivated by guilt, is built on exuberant rhetoric and dramatic symbols, and is nurtured by romantic idealism; and (5) university involvement gets entangled in ill-defined concepts of resident participation and community control.

Third, faculty and students who carry any responsibility for implementing service missions in depressed ghettos must constantly bear in mind three very essential facts. First, the concepts of resident participation and community control are important aspects of the culture of community action programs in the ghetto. Second, application of the concepts becomes sheer mockery and of dubious intent when ghetto residents are led to believe they exercise policy-control over their budgets, but do not in reality. Such a contradiction militates against the development of maturity, self-sufficiency, and fiscal accountability. Finally, one of the most valuable resources universities have for fulfilling their corporate citizenship obligation in the community, through public services, is their students. It is imperative, however, that any service students perform, as representatives of universities, be structured to advance educational goals. Otherwise, their experiences will continue to magnify the deficiencies which still characterize public service efforts by many universities—deficiencies which are rooted in romantic idealism, faulty conceptions, and inattention to the need for program structures that facilitate teaching and learning through service.

PART IV: COMMUNITY SERVICE MODELS

If universities undertake to render community services in depressed areas of a community, such services should be highly structured. This theory is reflected in the present organization of the urban affairs office. Critical structural elements are clearly defined in an operational manual that required fully a year to prepare. These elements include a clear statement of three broad functions of the program. The functions are: (1) it conducts research and encourages and supports research by other units of the university, to advance new knowledge concerning various aspects of the urban crisis; (2) it provides a base that permits greater participation in public action by members of the university community—action especially devoted to the improvement of service delivery in the community; and (3) on selected occasions it arranges experimental and short-term demonstration projects that enable faculty and students, in joint efforts with community groups, to develop and test new theories of, and approaches to, problem solving in the community.

This statement of functions is followed by descriptions that clearly show *how* these functions will be operationalized. They include: (1) a list of specific program areas, with definitions of recipients and the form and methods by which the program will be pursued; (2) clear description of the duties of each staff member, including student assistants and stenographers; (3) a schematic design which shows how the program ties in with the academic divisions of the university, with attention to feed-in and feedback; (4) a reiteration of program boundaries, e.g., education, research, and definitive public services; (5) a definition of the service unit in terms of its roles, e.g., encourager, energizer, enabler, supporter, broker, factfinder, consultant; and (6) a system for conducting continuous "in-house" evaluations of the program.

Another kind of model is also appropriate. Briefly, it would provide for a nonprofit agency that is situated between the community and the university. The agency would receive funds from the university, but would not be bound by university constraints, except for normal fiscal accountability. It would provide for full participation of both the university and the community in policy matters, program designing and implementation, and budgeting.

It would have the authority to grant community action groups full control over financial matters as the groups are found to be ready to operate with complete autonomy. This means that the agency must have "free money" in order to enable the groups to acquire experience in the area of fiscal management.

The agency would concentrate primarily on brokerage services. However, it would be equipped to assist community groups in other respects such as planning and implementing research designs, developing and implementing program models, training staff, developing operational structures, and conducting or assisting with program evaluations.

The agency would provide consultation to funding sources which may need assistance in determining if a community program is a good financial risk, and in determining ways in which community programs can be helped to reduce a risk status. The agency would especially concentrate on mobilizing resources which the university might have available to provide direct assistance to community groups in the previously mentioned areas of service. Consequently, it would have a faculty and student recruitment service and, also, a highly developed system of reward for university personnel who perform services. Such a system is necessary in order to ensure the highest quality of performance.

The agency should be staffed by an adequate complement of full-time personnel (the same requirements hold true for the other model). The following competencies should be present in the staff: ability to conduct pure and applied research; ability to raise money; ability to analyze human behavior and ecological patterns; ability to identify differing life styles and cultures endemic to various ethnic groups, especially racial minorities; ability to design and influence public policy; ability to conduct social planning; ability to design community-effective organization strategies; and the ability to develop management systems and budgetary structures. The full-time staff should not have other professional interests and obligations which require a diversion of attention and time from the primary job—diversions such as outside consultation, attending classes, teaching, or thesis preparation. Staff with such interests and obligations should be employed on a part-time or project-by-project basis in order to minimize the amount of interference with demands of the job. Experience has shown that many of the failures of university-based community service agencies are due in large part to situations where full-time staff have been diverted from the work of the agencies by demands upon staff time that are apart from the work of such agencies.

Finally, the agency should have a clearly defined culture that blends characteristics of both the community and the university, but where neither dominates the agency's mission. Actually, the envisaged agency is very similar to the consultant firms that emerged during the antipoverty era, except for three characteristics: (1) it would be nonprofit; (2) it would have a viable tie-in with universities, their central missions, and vast resources; and (3) it would provide free services to community groups who cannot afford to pay.

It is apparent that there are many mutual benefits to be derived from an active involvement of the university with its surrounding community. The involvement, however, needs to be developed out of an organizational base which allows a program to flourish. Insufficient regard for the problems of organization reflects our lack of systematic attention to the constraints and supports to be found in the social contexts in which programs are imbedded.

REFERENCES

Bard, M., and Berkowitz, B. Training police as specialists in family crisis intervention: A community psychology action program. *Community Mental Health Journal*, 1967, 3, 315–317.

Duff, R. S., and Hollingshead, A. B. *Sickness and society.* New York: Harper and Row, 1968.

Gardner, J. W. The university and the cities. *Educational Record,* (Winter) 1969.

Goldenberg, I. *Build me a mountain.* Cambridge, Mass.: The MIT Press, 1970.

Goldenberg, I., and Levine, M. The development and evolution of the Yale Psycho-Educational Clinic. *International Review of Applied Psychology,* 1969, 18, 100–101.

Joint Commission on Mental Illness and Health. *Action for mental health.* New York: Basic Books, 1961.

Kaplan, F., and Sarason, S. B. (Eds.). *The psycho-educational clinic: Papers and research studies.* Boston: Massachusetts Department of Mental Health, 1969.

Levine, M. Some postulates of practice in community psychology and their implications for training. In I. Iscoe and C. D. Spielberger (Eds.) *Community psychology: Perspectives in training and research.* New York: Appleton, Century-Crofts, 1970.

Levine, M., Dunn, F., Brochinsky, S., Bradley, J., and Donlan, K. Student teachers as tutors for children in an inner city school. *Child Psychology and Human Development,* 1970, 7, 50–56.

Levine, M., Wesolowski, J., and Corbett, F. Pupil turnover and academic performance in an inner-city elementary school. *Psychology in the Schools,* 1966, 3, 153–158.

Marris, P., and Rein, M. *Dilemmas of social reform.* New York: Atherton Press, 1967.

Moynihan, D. P. *Maximum feasible misunderstanding.* New York: Free Press, 1969.

Sarason, S. B. *The culture of the school and the problem of change.* Boston: Allyn and Bacon, 1971.

Sarason, S. B., and Levine, M. Graduate education and the Yale Psycho-Educational Clinic. In I. Iscoe and C. D. Spielberger (Eds.) *Community psychology: Perspec-*

tives in training and research. New York: Appleton, Century-Crofts, 1970.

Sarason, S. B., Levine, M., Goldenberg, I., Cherlin, D. C., and Bennett, E. *Psychology in community settings.* New York: Wiley, 1966.

State University of New York at Buffalo, Office of Urban Affairs. *Annual Report, 1970–1971.*

State University of New York at Buffalo, Office of Urban Affairs. *Organization of the Office of Urban Affairs,* 1971.

Wolfe, T. *Radical chic and mau-mauing the flak catchers.* New York: Farrar, Straus and Giroux, 1970.

9. The Relationship of the University to the Community: Implications for Community Mental Health Programs

I. IRA GOLDENBERG

INTRODUCTION

If I may, I should like in this paper to trouble you with what are, at least from my point of view, a few painful glimpses of the obvious. For purposes of brevity, let me list them now and then devote the remainder of this paper to the task of clarifying and exploring them. They are:

1. Contrary to the feelings (perhaps the hopes) of some people, the university and whatever we mean by "the community" are far more similar than they are different in terms of their over-all values, life styles, and systems of reward and punishment.

2. The core issue of our time, indeed the unresolved problem to which academically-based community psychology programs are supposed to address themselves—namely, the problem of oppression (defined as the causes, manifestations,

Paper presented at the American Psychological Association meetings in Washington, D.C., September 5, 1971.

and consequences of those forces, primarily institutional, which are inhibiting of healthy human development)—will never be dealt with until the issue of the university's internal moral credibility is given at least as much attention as the so-called mental health problems defined as residing "out there."

3. The advent of the community health movement, much like its now much-maligned predecessor, the War on Poverty, is fast becoming as much an attempt to rescue the university by camouflaging and cloaking it in a mantle of so-called relevance, as it is an attempt to develop the new knowledge needed to deal with the mental health problems of people living in what are now referred to as catchment areas.

4. To the degree that it is successful (i.e., takes the pressure off attempts to change the university), the community mental health movement will serve to perpetuate rather than change conditions of oppression, especially as they exist in the university.

In short, the central thesis of this paper is simple. It is that community psychology programs, located as they are primarily in universities, should not concern themselves exclusively with the community out there, but should, especially if they are to develop new knowledge and a sense of moral credibility, seek first to study and transform their own settings (i.e., the university and/or the community psychology program itself) from their present form into ones that are more liberating of people who work in them, more worthy of their respect, and more consistent, internally at least, with the rhetoric and prevailing conceptions of what a healthy community might be and how it might function. Put another way, let the generation of new knowledge and action begin at home where it is needed and where the data are most immediately available, rather than focus on other, external communities where the assumption is invariably made that we, who have not been able to deal effectively with the illness that pervades our own settings, possess both the skills and the right to help others lead more productive and mutually enhancing lives.

Having thus stated some conclusions, let me now backtrack and try to provide some of the data upon which they are based.

THE FLIGHT FROM THE UNIVERSITY

In 1965, I, together with a small group of so-called nonprofessionals from the inner-city of New Haven, Connecticut, became engaged in a process which eventually led to the development and implementation of something called the Residential Youth Center (RYC). The RYC, which became operational in 1966, was a neighborhood-based, indigenously-staffed facility whose public mission was to work with those youth (aged 16 to 21) termed incorrigible by most of the established social, legal, and mental health related agencies. In addition, the RYC was to address itself to several other issues including:

—the feasibility of a setting ostensibly devoted to problems of individual remediation becoming actively engaged in problems of institutional change and social intervention;
—the degree to which such a setting, directed and manned almost exclusively by so-called nonprofessionals, could handle the kinds of clinical problems previously considered to be solely within the jurisdiction and competence of mental health professionals; and
—the possibility of such a setting serving as a community-based training and research facility for gradu-

ate students preparing for careers in the field of community mental health.

However, its public mandate and contractual goals notwithstanding, it soon became clear that many of us involved in the project had become a part of the group for reasons only tangentially related to the desire to develop more meaningful and innovative services for disadvantaged youth. This is not to say or to imply that such motivations were unimportant. In a very real sense we were certainly responding to and honestly caught up in the sense of purpose that pervaded the early and middle Sixties. As we have written elsewhere,

> The year was 1965, and it was a time when America was forcing itself to look inward toward its own problems, its own people, and its own institutions. The New Frontier, although born out of neither innocence nor empty idealism, was capturing the young and recapturing the old and providing both with a renewed sense of history. A country was stirring, beginning to move, and reawakening in its citizens those feelings of commitment and action that in preceding years had either lain dormant because of fear or been channeled into the frantic quest for security, sameness or personal oblivion. But more than anything else, there was a climate of hope, a feeling of identity, and a belief that man could again begin to control his own destiny and create a society that was more rational, liberating, and worthy of its people. (Goldenberg, 1971).

As indicated previously, however, for many of us the decision to become involved in the development of a new setting was also determined by other, far less altruistic reasons. More concretely, we were both as individuals and as a group, far from happy (often increasingly bitter) in the settings, programs, or institutions in which we were already engaged and from which we earned our livelihoods. Thus, whether we were Assistant Professors at an Ivy League school, truck drivers, rock 'n roll singers, ex-policemen, or employees of the local community action agency, we were people who had begun to become increasingly concerned about the relationship between how we were leading our lives and the context of the values and life styles that dominated the settings in which we were employed. Put another way, each of us, independent of our varying skills, interests, levels of formal education or particular competencies, had arrived at that point in time when questions concerning the quality of life—the quality of our own lives—could no longer be separated from the nature and ideologies of the systems of which we were a part. What became increasingly clear were two things. First, that we were all, in one way or another, fleeing from settings which, despite their rhetoric, were essentially sick and often dehumanizing in terms of their prevailing conceptions of man and the accompanying internal structures they had developed in order to perpetuate and protect those conceptions. And second, that the primary goal in developing the RYC would, of necessity, be much less directly related to problems of service and much more related to the issues posed in trying to develop a setting in which we, no differently than our clients, would begin to feel increasingly self-determining and, for want of a better word, healthier. In short, what had supposedly begun as an attempt to rehabilitate others was quickly transformed into a project whose initial focus was to develop for its rehabilitators a setting that was very different from the ones out of which they themselves had recently emerged.

Now, without going into great detail about the RYC itself, let me sketch briefly some of the issues that had to be dealt with once it became clear that what we were really engaged in was the attempt to develop a setting whose degree of internal health provided its members with the experience, skills, and moral credibility to even presume to lay on others alternative ways of dealing with the forces that mitigate against healthy human development.

To begin with, there was the problem posed whenever people of different races—let alone people with varying backgrounds, levels of formal education, and socially reinforced labels—try to develop a common ground and ideology to guide their actions. Issues that are all too often ignored or presumed to have minimal interference potential cannot be dismissed. The myth of men of good will acting in concert with each other despite long-standing fears and patterns of mutual distrust—that self-deluding guiding fiction that pervades so many attempts (and misattempts) at social reform—becomes exactly what it is, a myth whose destructive potential can rarely be overemphasized. *Racism* (and its accompanying conscious and unconscious correlates) is always an issue, ever present and constantly confronting people with the categorical imperative of dealing with its consequences, particularly in terms of their own interactions, political stances, and interpersonal behavior.

A second issue had to do with the question of *power and leadership,* what they meant and how they ought to be exercised in the setting. As was the case with respect to racism, public rhetoric could no longer replace the development of tangible alternatives to a system in which the few, often for reasons unrelated to competence or special talent, exercise inordinate power over the many for whom and about whom there are then developed elaborate institutional and psychological rationales that both reinforce and confirm the need for power being centralized in the hands of some essentially unchanging elitist group.

Closely related to the issue of power was the question of the nature of the *decision-making process* that would characterize the setting. How would decisions be made? By whom? And on what basis? Again the issue of roles, assumptions concerning commitment, competence, and the willingness of people to share very concrete functions and responsibilities had to be explored in new ways, in ways unrelated to traditional conceptions of expertise and formal training.

And finally, there was the question of *cooperation;* real cooperation in a setting composed of people who had previously been regarded, be it in the community or in the university, for their ability and adroitness at competing with and manipulating others. The issue here was almost frighteningly simple: could a group of people coming from settings in which the rhetoric of cooperation was always systematically undercut by the reality of reward systems that reinforced the development of competitive life-styles begin to develop the kind of personal and political consciousness that would enable them to transcend their own socialization processes?

Time and space do not permit me to dwell extensively with the results of this natural experiment in the creation of a setting. I think, however, that it would be fair to say that none of us who were a part of it, either as residents or staff, emerged from the experience untouched or unchanged. The process of development as well as the results of the Residential Youth Center have been presented in a variety of different publications. I might add that although a book recently published about the RYC has been rather favorably reviewed in a number of different journals (including some of our traditional "liberal" ones), I have been struck by how little attention reviewers have paid to some of the issues I have tried to outline here, even though these issues easily comprise two-thirds of the book's contents. It seems, rather, that reviewers, perhaps no differently than those of us officially perceived as involved in matters of community mental health, feel much more comfortable focusing attention on questions concerning clinical results for and on the target population than on the institutional and political implications of a setting developed, as the RYC was, as a reaction against the prevailing conceptions and internal processes that characterize most of our university departments and community agencies.

WHY NOT THE UNIVERSITY AS CLIENT?

Having said all this, let me turn to the university as the setting in which most community mental health programs are either located physically, or to which they look for both intellectual sustenance and future professional manpower.

The university, no differently than the ghetto, the police department, the State Employment Service, or any other psycho-geographically defined area or institution, consists of a complex series of interlocking (though by no means mutual) interests—interests defined over time and invested with a degree of apparent, if not actual, validity. Its composition bespeaks a delicate balance of power groups, institutional relationships, and spheres of influence. Each segment may bring with it some slightly altered view of the world; but together they define the university as a community, give it its uniqueness, shape its pattern of enduring values and traditions, and share in its perpetuation. In short, when all is said and done, the university—be it through the definition of research it considers to be scholarly, its departmental decisions concerning tenure, the models of interpersonal relations it makes available to its faculty and students, or the manner in which it deals with that most political of supposedly non-political concepts, academic freedom—both defines a way of life and sets the limits, both political and intellectual, of acceptable and unacceptable deviance (Tussman, 1969; Farber, 1968).

Now, if we take a look at the university from the point of view of its function as another setting in which the process of socialization, begun in early childhood and continued through a variety of educational institutions, is carried on even further, a few things become relatively clear. The first is that the university, like so many other institutions in our society, is currently being confronted with the reality that despite its theoretical if not physical separation from the world, it has not escaped the forces, both external and internal, that have rendered it an often oppressive and ideologically constricting setting. The very same problems that supposedly define life on the outside exist within. Problems related to poverty, racism, sexism, and the legitimate and illegitimate uses of power are as much a part of the university as they are of those settings and institutions labeled as existing in the community (Benne, 1970). Furthermore, it becomes uncomfortably clear that the quality of human relationships within the university is no more or less healthy than those typically encountered elsewhere, in settings unencumbered by the rhetoric of growth, freedom, and the pursuit of one's own thing. It is, in short, a picture of the university as both reflector and perpetuator of a social ethos whose roots run deep and are inextricably bound up in the American experience. The university, for all its attempts at social detachment and political disinterest, emerges as another setting which both echoes and is afflicted by those unresolved problems which currently threaten the very fabric of what we know of as the American society. From a clinical point of view, one could not ask for a more worthy client in need of help.

COMMUNITY PSYCHOLOGY PROGRAMS

Let us now turn, finally, to the functions and purposes of community psychology programs, particularly those that are university-based and charged with the responsibility of developing the manpower, knowledge, theoretical conceptions, and research methodologies to be used in dealing with problems of community mental health. To begin with, we might point out that the growth of the community mental health movement—the movement most directly responsible for the development of academically-based programs in the area of community psychology—was a response to the growing evidence indicating that existing models of clinical functioning were grossly inadequate both in meeting the need for services and in providing services that were effective (Joint Commission on Mental Illness and Health, 1961). Moreover, it was finally recognized that an inordinate amount of human misery was somehow caused, exacerbated by, or connected with the functioning of a variety of social and economic institutions (e.g., schools, welfare and employment settings, etc.) which, when taken together, exercise enormous power in determining the quality of life in any given community and for any given group of people (Albee, 1959; Goldenberg and Levine, 1969). Their inadequacies, whether by design or by accident, had as much to do with generating the conditions for mental and emotional dysfunctioning as did the unresolved problems traditionally associated with conflict-ridden psycho-sexual development. Thus, if not by public mandate, then certainly by the logic dictated by existing data, community psychology programs have to address themselves to at least two issues traditionally alien to most mental health professionals. The first has to do with an analysis and understanding of the dominative structures of our society and their accompanying underlying ideological assumptions about man, the human condition, and change. The second involves the often painful search for and creation of more liberating forms or arrangements of those institutions, be they social, educational, or political, that significantly affect human growth and development. In short, community psychology programs, whether they wish to admit it or not, are charged with the responsibility of utilizing their traditional concern for and knowledge about the individual to alter if possible, or to develop anew if necessary, our most basic institutions. This is no small task for a profession (or scientific discipline) which brings with it to the task a social legacy not too different from the one it is now asked to question and change.

Some Implications

So where does this leave us? I think it leaves us at a point in time when those of us involved in the development of academically-based community psychology programs have to make some crucial decisions—decisions about ourselves, our own settings, our own aspirations, and our own willingness to reorder what have already become traditional community psychology and community mental health programs. More specifically, it implies the following:

1. That we begin to take very seriously the sociopolitical implications of the conditions which gave rise to the community mental health movement in the first place.
2. That we begin to devote our time and energy to the task of developing alternative institutional models in which the rhetoric accompanying the concept of community mental health is translated into a viable internal reality rather than some on-going mythology that is, at once, both soothing to its creators and infuriating to people in the community.
3. That we commit ourselves to studying, understanding, and changing our own settings (i.e., the university), and to accepting the risks that will invariably follow all such attempts.

Having gone this far and given the problems as I've tried to define them, I would feel much better if I could end this brief paper with some reasonable predictions of success. Unfortunately, given the nature of most universities and psychology departments I cannot in all good conscience offer any. The problems inherent in any thoroughgoing attempt to deal constructively and creatively with the sources, manifestations, and consequences of oppression in any of its forms, either within or outside of the university, are too numerous to permit the forecasting of positive results. If, however, such attempts are undertaken, and if they should succeed, we will not only have succeeded in generating the new knowledge and institutional models so desperately needed in the field, but we will also have succeeded, at the very least, in making it unnecessary for people to flee the university in order to rekindle for themselves elsewhere that sense of self-determination that is so much a part of the experience of health. If, on the other hand, such attempts fail (as well they may), those who were a part of them will have at least failed with a modicum of grace. In either event, the one guarantee that can be offered is that, as was the case with those of us involved in the creation of the Residential Youth Center, none who are a part of it will emerge from the experience untouched or unchanged. Perhaps, in the final analysis, that is the most important thing of all.

REFERENCES

Albee, G. W. *Mental health manpower trends.* New York: Basic Books, 1959.

Benne, K. D. Authority in education. *Harvard Educational Review,* 1970, 40, 385–410.

Farber, G. Student as Nigger. *Daily Bruin Spectra,* UCLA, April 4, 1967.

Goldenberg, I. I. *Build me a mountain: Youth, poverty, and the creation of new settings.* Cambridge: MIT Press, 1971.

Goldenberg, I. I., and Levine, M. The development and evolution of the Yale Psycho-Educational Clinic. *International Review of Applied Psychology,* 1969, 18.

Joint Commission on Mental Illness and Health. *Action for mental health.* New York: Basic Books, 1961.

Tussman, J. *Experiment at Berkeley.* Oxford: Oxford University Press, 1969.

Part IV

A SOCIAL PSYCHIATRIST'S POINT OF VIEW

10. *The University and the Urban Crisis*

LEONARD J. DUHL

My concern in this paper is with the university; but it is also with our society and where it is now going. To try to separate the university or society from myself, and the changes that have taken place within me, is a difficult and almost impossible task. Thus, I ask you to bear with me, as I relate something of my own education, and try to point out where I am today as a professor in a major American university.

The pathway to professorship was through medicine, psychiatry, and psychoanalysis. Out of this educational and professional experience came concern not only with the individual who needs help, but a commitment to the needs of population groups who are only partially served by our human services, either out of lack of knowledge or power to get what they want and need or because of basic inequities in the system of service. For many years, serving as a Washington bureaucrat, I helped support universities, in research and training, while faced all too often with their inability to meet the needs of the society. How futile it was to ask for help from universities on major social programs; how distant from policy issues, and how unreal was their reaction to social change and the needs of new students.

When I entered the university as a faculty member in a program in social policy planning I had already served as a national planner in mental health, fought battles in the Office of Education Research Advisory Committee as a member, asked for help to HUD as a top level HUD staff man, and had participated in the creation of numerous "Golden Era" national programs: Peace Corps, Poverty, Model Cities, Mental Retardation.

With this background I became a professional educator, and I asked myself as I began the new role: What was education all about? A tremendous influx of new students with mixed backgrounds and experience inundated the university. Those who "knew where they were at" went to and found the established departments. Those looking for a moratorium—or a chance to find their identity—went to the new programs. An emerging new program is one where the identity is not set. City Planning, building on past physical planning and economic analytic bases, was in turmoil over social planning and advocacy—and thus an ideal place for searching students of varied psychological and career profiles to go. Public Health, in the midst of similar changes from epidemiological laboratory to medical care, was wide open, and students with varied concerns for ecology, social health, medical services, and social reform entered in abundance.

All similar programs fared in the same way. In schools like Berkeley, torn by the torments of student rebellion and reactive conservatism, the massive cafeteria of courses overwhelms the student who tries to put together a personalized "gourmet" meal. Surely the same question of integrating the vast number of pieces and parts which make up knowledge has always been with us, but the input of students—or users—was previously a more select sample of our population. (By select I mean able to know exactly where he was going, what slot he was aiming for, what was needed to achieve those goals, and possessing an ability to synthesize the parts into what he felt was a relevant whole.)

Consider then the dilemma of a university. It must deal with:

—A vast input of variously prepared, motivated, and directed students.

—Unknown goals of its products, since the world for which the university prepares them is changing faster than the university's capability to deliver.

—Great numbers of students needing "processing"— where faculty-student ratios have been going down and where neither the faculty nor the administration are willing or able to assist in the role of helping the student find a unique path for himself and a future role which would aid in society's search for new solutions to its problems.

—The university as an institution, quite naturally finding it as difficult to change as any individual faced by inevitable truths about himself, to find new patterns of behavior. People and institutions are inherently conservative, less by choice than by biological, social, and psychological processes which tend more easily toward "sclerosis" than toward innovation.

—The ever-deepening crises that arise from confronting piecemeal the varied parts of the university requiring changing. As a result, the university relies on adaptive responses rather than on critical or major reorientation of structure and process.

What I have noted about the university can be seen in the society at large. The university is the city in microcosm; no longer the contained, hierarchical organization with clearly defined purposes but a former "multiversity" faced with hundreds of independent parts each doing their own thing and subjected to the whims and vicissitudes of all political structures: power fights, turf battles, patronage, and vicious infighting we see in cities (perhaps more openly because the stakes are smaller).

The city, as Webber (1968) has pointed out, is no more. It is a noncity—a collection of homogeneous places connected together by a web of arbitrary rules, freeways, and governances into a thing called a city (Los Angeles!). Where are its boundaries? Who is in charge? Is there coherence, control, or leadership? University administrators are buffeted like mayors by the whims of riot and confrontation, the press, and TV; major decisions affecting the institution's life are made arbitrarily without concern for the whole or the long run. How easy it is to pick a president who is low profile and will not rock the boat, and who will not face the realities of the world but will only hold together a rocking (sinking) ship (Bennis, 1971).

The "nonuniversity" contains the important remnants of the past: the preservation of knowledge, science, and objective analysis of the world—pieces I cannot do without. Yet it is also faced by the new demands and crisis— "to be relevant" and to meet the flood of new "immigrants" ill-prepared for citizenship.

The A+ universities can face this demand two ways:

> —"We are there; thus we can attempt to test ourselves and try new roles both within and outside the walls" (Brewster and Yale).
> —"We must pull back and protect our flanks because our life blood is dependent on not disturbing the source of our funds" (state universities).

The aspiring universities can only face up to their image of the top ten (real or imagined) and take few risks, while the bread-and-butter colleges faced by torment can only grow (like some urban universities) or succumb to mediocrity and the past.

In all—with varied pressures—the demands of the community, students, faculty (sometimes), and administration may add up to change despite themselves. The external form remains the same while the quality of the courses and programs almost unconsciously transmit a new ethos.

As a psychiatrist I am so often struck by the need to "save face," remaining the same (the same old U.S. Constitution) with new interpretations, and even an anti-change mentality which nevertheless communicates "silent, covert messages to the viewers." The television stories and news coverage which attack radicalism and confrontation nevertheless communicate a new ethos and value system far beyond our ability to control. The effect of the "music of the young"—censured by FCC regulations on mentioning drugs—can only with its complete (and impossible) suppression stop communicating a new ethos.

The university is in this situation: no matter how its official structure and curriculum communicates, a vast new competitive education system of wall newspapers, the underground press, music, and the word-of-mouth communication by rumor and via telephone, travel, and informal get-togethers, is affecting the minds of those students heretofore the private precinct of the university machinery to educate to a degree. That this is occurring, concurrently with attempts to remain with Consciousness II, is neither an argument for the Reichian (Reich, 1970) nor conservative models. Rather it argues for changes in the unconscious, while the conscious remains unchanged but tormented; it portends change in following generations who cannot help but hear the covert as well as overt message.

The university's role (or one of them) is to transmit knowledge and to assist in preparing people for the immediate future. There are then at least two roles it must take:

—The search for knowledge about who and what we are, were, and are becoming.
—A need to face problems, rather than disciplines or professions. This role is not new to the university,

for it has done just this in agriculture, medicine, business, and national defense. What is new is a reordering of priorities, with issues concerning people becoming more important than things.

In the move toward problems, classical positions of the university come under attack. Even though universities realize they can never destroy what already exists in program and curriculum, they nevertheless fight the added programs which may meet new demands (the orthodox faculties, I'm sure, fought the inroads of science; some I know preferred not to have practical programs such as medicine or even law in their orbit, in the not too distant past). The arguments are diverse and polarization results.

My concern is not the abolition of what is, nor the systematic institution of controls (a PPBS solution), for in either case we limit the number of options open. At this moment in time any fixing of the question of what is the university cannot help but limit future options and choices. I am thus against either pole. Rather I would encourage the maximum number of options (mini-universities) within the whole, which would assist the student to put together the diverse ways unique to his own needs and the community's requirements.

To divorce the uniqueness of the student—or indeed my own perception of who I am and what I need—from the question of the *roles* of a university would be a sad state of affairs. Hopefully, we—not knowing what the future will bring (since our projections into the future always fail due to constant value and ideological shifts)—will create a true noncity of learning, a university of diversity and dispersion, where new patterns of education will be attempted (Freedman, 1971; Duhl, 1970) and no model fixed in perpetuity.

This then becomes the moment for advocacy—a statement of what I see needed and an attempt to claim "one piece of the pot" in the large university universe (its budget?).

Since our society is in flux and there are *no* answers to our pressing problems—only muddling towards possible solutions—we have to open ourselves to experiment. Our focus must be directed towards how our society operates and how to change it. Simplifying our needs we can see levels of concern about human behavior (independent of current disciplines): (a) the individual, family, and group; (b) the organization (public and private); and (c) government and politics.

In each we must truly begin to understand (not theoretically but by translation into action) something about the realities of society's current behavior. It is neither good nor bad; it operates pragmatically with a veneer of ideology, with patronage and corruption, "white collar crime," the ins and outs varying with ascension to power no matter what the ideology, with fear, selfishness, concern for our private turf, the need to preserve what is, and the apathetic acceptance of all this as a way of life. No matter how hard we sell new images of the world, the ordinary citizen is carried by short-run concerns (even professors) and bread-and butter issues whether they be money, happiness, accomplishment, or kicks.

Against this knowledge of what is (raw, anthropolitical, muckraking in the style of Lincoln Steffins and Albert Deutsch) must be placed the knowledge we have about change. How hard it is to admit that active interventions may have little long-run impact and only momentary diversion of the stream of societal and individual change. How many of us brave Kennedy "world changers" see how unimportant our role was in the nature of things. How sad is the result of psychotherapy evaluation which, like radical and reform movements, operates more on faith and input measures than the result of outputs.

We can say for sure, however, that people who participate in their own salvation—fighting for changes in things that affect their lives—feel better, have a sense of integrity and worth. We know too that those who feel they belong—to family, tribe, collegial "floating crap game," or invisible college[1]—have a security which permits identity to form and an integrity to develop.

Thus the knowledge of change—its theories and techniques—critical to knowledge transmission is also central to the structure of the educational organization itself. Whether the problem is change or evaluation of change the focal issue may be men's relation to each other. The central question may be the infrastructure of governance rather than the pieces and parts; the linkage, the synthesis, and integration instead of individual disciplines and skills (Duhl, 1967).

What does this suggest for the university structure itself? The nonuniversity university may well become not a purveyor of pieces of knowledge but an integrator and synthesizer. This role may be performed inside the university or in the new nonuniversity university: by individuals, the institutes, consulting firms, and knowledge factories. What happens in these groups?

People within it (perpetual students) draw upon ideas, courses, and people from a variety of places located either within or outside the university proper. Faced with real life tasks (performed for better or worse) they pull together, independent of discipline, whatever is needed for the job. Ideas are integrated, people learn to synthesize, use analog thinking (Schon, 1963, 1967), and develop creative innovative approaches to old issues. Unhampered by tradition, free of the security questions plaguing tenured and untenured faculties, they can produce irreverent and nonexpected responses.

Indeed, many new approaches towards groups (T-groups, encounter groups) and budget control (PPBS) among many others have come not from established universities but from the new think tank, consultation organization "universities." Such questions as hierarchy

---

[1]See Leonard J. Duhl, "Social Values, Politics, and Health in Governance—The Metropolitan Family" to be published by Resources for the Future in a book, edited by Charles M. Haar, on Metropolitan Development.

versus collegial models become easier. The nature of scientific research, for example, can be tested.

For example, it is my strong belief that the critical issues of research are within the context of man's interrelationship to man, institutions, and even machines. It is the processes of interaction, the linkage questions, both formal and informal, which are critical. The nature of research shifts, especially when the variables are unclear and when values change. Man's appreciative system (Vickers, 1965) becomes unable to comprehend in old ways, and he requires new techniques for governance and integration of what "he knows." Research may require more anthropolitical incursions into situations, permitting theory to emerge (Blumer, 1969) rather than to control studies. The more standard scientific inquiry techniques may not hold in this situation.

What then for structure? A shift towards education rather than training would recognize our inability to predict the future. A form of integrating basic knowledge with experiential knowledge recognizes that both *in vivo* and *in vitro* experiments are needed. Educating people from multiple disciplines together reflects real life issues. Linking psychological with social and cognitive learning reflects an understanding of human behavior.

It is on this last point that I would like to dwell. The students I have seen who come not with prescribed notions of what their role is, but with a need for a moratorium where they can find their unique future, require help which ofttimes is not forthcoming. Often their personal solutions are fortuitous depending on the faculty member they work with. They are lost in the "cafeteria" and the implosive demands of diverse societal inputs and need assistance.

I have called for "therapeutic communities" as education models, knowing that the word "therapy" has negative connotations. Rather my concern is with "intentional communities" who gather for the moment (a new tribalism)[2] to share, transmit, assist, and educate each other on mutually shared problems. The old definitions fail. Who is teacher and student? Where are the walls of university? Are the consumers teachers or clients? All these questions and others challenge us.

By proposing this model I *do not* condemm the university as we know it to obsolescence; rather I'd like to use its offerings and resources in a new manner. But to do so requires a new notion of educational experience: in my mini-university (and there must be others with different goals) people concerned with problems (sociologists, doctors, planners, lawyers, psychologists, economists, and many others) must be blended with integrative "specialists in generalization," and those concerned with bringing out the psychological best in people,[3] as well as social experiential learning. Carl Rogers' *Freedom to Learn* (1969), the encounter group movement, and even the communes are models—not to be followed in toto—but which *suggest* the components of a system of learning which encourages diverse student input and output and which can produce usable products in assisting social change in our institutions and government.

I can easily be accused of trying to create change agents and not scholars. I can only retort that the scholars and researchers I want are those who are concerned (in my proposed mini-university) with societal change and can give us answers not to basic research but to action-oriented issues. The clinician model in medicine, with its research base, is one model, focusing on issues of diagnosis, intervention, and evaluation, despite limited knowledge (heresy?). This is said despite my own critique of "the medical model," which in its classical usage is unaware of the human ecological issues of man and his envi-

---

[2]See Peter Marris' book on African entrepreneurship, to be published.
[3]See Michael Burns' not too complete study of Finchden Manor—a program for adolescents, "Mr. Lyward's Answer," Beacon Press.

ronment. This issue aside, my push is closer to the professions as models than academia.

The days ahead of us seem to me to offer three options: (a) a continued nightmare (e.g., Bourne, *et al.*, 1971); (b) a tight rationalized systematic control system where we think we "know" what the outputs are; or (c) a new system of planned diversity which permits nonrationality (not irrationality) and multiple attempts at solution-finding for society.

Since the university is a reflection of society—and indeed reacts rather than leads (as some think it has and should)—it is in the process of great change. If it resists change, it may be our twentieth or twenty-first century dinosaur; or more likely it will maintain its label but give up its function to newly emerging parts of our society which uniquely are the new education institutions.[4]

In sum, our search is for competence, in the individual and in our institutions (public and private) to be able to command events that affect our lives. The basic poverty (Seeley, 1967) of our society is in our failure to meet the pressures for change either in ourselves or in our organizations by coping, adapting, growing, or being "self-renewing" (Gardner, 1964, 1970a, 1970b). Since our societal crisis—our urban crisis—is our university crisis, it may be ludicrous to ask a crisis-ridden institution to create the conditions for its own salvation. But indeed we must; for whether it be university, community group, or government, that is the only place that salvation lies.

I turn to the university—perhaps unjustifiably—since my respect for learning and education was bred into me so long ago (indeed it was culturally conditioned) in hopes that it can perform a unique role: critic, leader, educator, even therapist. Yet I also know it can't, but it can in its

---

[4]This is not an argument for the free schools to replace the school system; rather that it be one set of mini-schools within a diverse system that permits, encourages, and responds to confrontations that come from new solutions (Berkeley Public Schools).

parts (and this is what I am advocating); and its members and its products can be part of a bigger search for solution in the broader society and in new education institutions. This is an awesome challenge to the reader and to myself.

REFERENCES

Bennis, W. G. Searching for the 'perfect' university president. *Atlantic Monthly, 1971.*

Blumer, H. *Symbolic interactionism—perspective and method.* Englewood Cliffs, N. J.: Prentice-Hall, 1969.

Bourne, P., *et al.* Day care nightmare. Institute of Urban and Regional Development, University of California, Berkeley, February, 1971.

Duhl, L. J. Planning and predicting: Or what to do when you don't know the names of the variables. *Daedalus,* Vol. 96, No. 3, Summer 1967.

Duhl, L. J. The university and service to the community. *Experiment and Innovation: New Directions in Education at the University of California,* Vol. 3, No. 1, 1970.

Freedman, L. The progress report of the president's task force on the extended university. University of California at Los Angeles, March 12, 1971.

Gardner, J. *Self-renewal—The individual and the innovative society.* New York: Harper & Row, 1964.

Gardner, J. *No easy victories.* New York: Harper & Row, 1970.(a)

Gardner, J. *Recovery of confidence.* New York: Harper & Row, 1970.(b)

Reich, C. *The greening of America.* New York: Random House, 1970.

Rogers, C. *Freedom to learn.* New York: Bobbs Merrill, 1969.

Schon, D. *Invention and the evolution of ideas.* New York: Barnes & Noble, 1963.

Schon, D. *Technology and change.* New York: Dell publishing Co., 1967.

Seeley, J. *Americanization of the unconscious.* New York: International Science Press, 1967.

Vickers, G. *The art of judgment.* Basic Books, 1965.

Webber, M. The post-city age. *Daedalus,* Fall, 1968.

Part V

POINTS AND COUNTERPOINTS

11. Facts About Philadelphia and its Institutions of Higher Learning

PATRICIA L. ROSENBAUM

FACTS ABOUT PHILADELPHIA

Philadelphia's population patterns for the last twenty years have resembled those of other major American metropolitan areas: the SMSA (Standard Metropolitan Statistical Area) grew by over one million people while the center city's population declined slightly. Suburban population rose by nearly 80 percent during the same time. The black population grew at a much faster rate than did the white, reflecting both a higher birth rate and immigration from the South.

TABLE 1
Total and Black Population of the Philadelphia Area 1950–1970

Year	Metropolitan Area	City of Philadelphia
Total Population		
1950	3,671,048	2,071,605
1970	4,817,914	1,948,609
Black Population		
1950	480,075	376,041
1970	844,300	653,791

Source: 1950, 1970 U.S. Census

In 1950, slightly more than half (53.1 percent) of the white population of the SMSA resided in center city along with almost 80 percent (78.3) of the black population. In 1970, almost the same percentage (77.4) of the black population still resided in center city but the white population had dropped to one-third (32.6 percent) of the total white population of the SMSA.

Incomes of center-city Philadelphia residents have not kept up with incomes of residents of the total SMSA, or of the state as a whole. The gap between median SMSA income and median city income now amounts to some $1,500. In 1970, income for black families was lower than income for total families in Philadelphia: $7,379 compared with $9,366.

The Puerto Rican population of Philadelphia has been increasing in recent years; there are strong indications that proportionately even more Puerto Ricans than blacks went uncounted in the most recent census. The census figure of 26,702 is estimated by community leaders to be only one-fourth to one-third the actual community size. On every measure, Philadelphia's Puerto Rican population shows up as more disadvantaged than the black population.

In educational attainment during the twenty-year period, Philadelphia showed a smaller increase in the median years of schooling than did the SMSA, the state, or the nation as a whole. The slow growth of educational attainment was also reflected in the increase in numbers of those who had completed high school and/or four years of college.

Pennsylvania's record of financial support for education is mixed. HEW reports indicate Pennsylvania's total expenditures for public schools as a percentage of personal income were almost exactly the same proportion (5.48) as national figures (5.46). However, this comparison ignores the large number of pupils in the parochial school system: in Philadelphia one-third of the school-age population attends nonpublic schools. Where higher education is concerned, Pennsylvania shows up very badly. In 1967–68 only four states spent a lower percentage of personal income on higher education than did Pennsylvania (and New Hampshire): .50 of 1 percent. The U.S. average was .75 of 1 percent.

FACTS ABOUT PHILADELPHIA'S
INSTITUTIONS OF HIGHER LEARNING

More than fifty institutions of higher education are located in the Philadelphia area, ranging in type from junior colleges to universities. Numbered among them are: the first university to use that name—the University of Pennsylvania; one of the country's largest universities —Temple University; the oldest Hebrew teacher-training institution in the western hemisphere; a variety of professional and technical schools; and some of the nation's finest liberal arts colleges.

TABLE 2
Percent Completing Specified Educational Levels 1950–1970

	Over 25 with 4+ yrs. H.S.		Over 25 with 4+ yrs. College	
	1950	1970	1950	1970
Philadelphia City	28.0	39.9	4.7	6.8
SMSA	32.3	50.6	6.2	10.7
State	33.7	50.2	5.4	8.8
U.S.	33.4	55.3	6.0	11.1

Source: 1950, 1970 U.S. Census

As the individual descriptions will show, most of the liberal arts colleges in the Philadelphia area were originally established by various religious groups, although most are not sectarian today. This reflects the early history of education generally in Pennsylvania; educational institutions at every level were initially developed by religious groups. Institutions supported by public funds were a later development on Pennsylvania's educational scene; publicly-funded community colleges were not introduced in Pennsylvania until the early 1960's.

Many institutions of higher education in the Philadelphia area are still supported by private sources. There are several state colleges which are owned and operated by the state. There are seven community colleges funded by state, local, and student funds, and branches of the state universities of Pennsylvania and New Jersey. In addition to state-owned colleges, Pennsylvania has two other types of relationships which provide financial support from state funds to institutions of higher education. Temple University and Lincoln University along with the Pennsylvania State University are "state-related"; they receive state grants for operations and experience a certain amount of state control such as state appointments to their Boards of Trustees. A number of other institutions, most of them technical or professional schools, are "state-aided"; they are private institutions receiving direct allocations for specific purposes from the state legislature. Pennsylvania is the only state to offer this latter type of support for higher education.

Following is a listing of institutions of higher learning in the Delaware Valley (five counties in Pennsylvania and three in New Jersey). They are divided by state and type· General; Special, Technical, and Professional; Junior Colleges; Community Colleges.

PENNSYLVANIA

General

Beaver College.   Enrollment (1972): 794 women. Beaver is a private, nonsectarian, liberal arts college, related to the United Presbyterian Church in the USA. Founded in 1853, it has a suburban campus and its student body is largely residential. It has an undergraduate program offering the B.A., B.S., and B.F.A.

Bryn Mawr College.   Enrollment (1972): 790 under-graduate women, 450 graduate men and women. Bryn Mawr is a private, nondenominational, liberal arts school established by the Society of Friends. Founded in 1885, it has a suburban campus. Its undergraduate program, for women only, offers the B.A.; its coeducational graduate programs offer the M.S.S., M.A., and Ph.D.

Cabrini College.   Enrollment (1972): 349 women, 13 men. Cabrini is a private, liberal arts, Catholic college. Founded in 1957, it has a suburban campus. It is residential for women only but takes men as day students. It has an undergraduate program offering the B.A., B.S., and B.S.Ed.

Chestnut Hill College.   Enrollment (1972): 650 women. This is a private, Catholic, liberal arts school. Founded in 1924, its campus is located in residential Philadelphia. Its undergraduate program offers the B.A. and B.S.

Cheyney State College.   Enrollment (1972): 1100 men, 1200 women. This is a state-owned, liberal arts school, oriented toward training teachers. It was originally established as a teachers college. Its student body is 85% black. Founded in 1837, it has a rural campus. It has both under-graduate and graduate programs; undergraduate degrees offered are the B.A. and B.S.Ed

Drexel University.   Enrollment (1972): 4238 men, 1069 women. Drexel is a private, state-aided institution, oriented toward science and technology. Founded in 1891, it has a West Philadelphia city campus It offers both undergraduate and graduate programs; the undergraduate program leads to the B.S.

Eastern College. Enrollment (1972): 270 men, 289 women. Eastern is a private, liberal arts school associated with the American Baptist Convention. Formerly Eastern Baptist College, it has a suburban campus. Its undergraduate program offers the B.A.

Gwynned-Mercy College. Enrollment (1972): 1057 women. This is a private, liberal arts, Catholic school. Founded in 1948, its campus is located in a suburban-rural area north of Philadelphia. Its program is undergraduate and offers the B.A. and B.S.

Haverford College. Enrollment (1972): 700 men. Haverford is a private, liberal arts college established by the Society of Friends. Founded in 1833, the first college established by the Friends, it has a suburban campus. Its program is undergraduate, offering the B.A. and B.S.; it exchanges classes with Bryn Mawr College.

Holy Family College. Enrollment (1972): 345 women. This is a private, liberal arts, Catholic school. Founded in 1954, it is located in residential Philadelphia. It has an undergraduate program offering the B.S.

Immaculata College. Enrollment (1972): 760 women. Immaculata is a private, Catholic, liberal arts school. Founded in 1920, it has a suburban-rural campus west of Philadelphia. Its program is undergraduate and offers the B.A. and B.S.

LaSalle College. Enrollment (1972): 3069 men, 623 women. LaSalle is a private, liberal arts, Catholic school. It has recently become coeducational. Founded in 1863, it has an north-central city campus. It has an undergraduate program offering the B.A. and B.S.B.A.

Lincoln University. Enrollment (1972): 639 men, 439 women. Lincoln is a state-related, nonsectarian, liberal arts school. The student body is largely black. Its campus is located in a rural area 45 miles west of Philadelphia. It has an undergraduate program offering the B.A.

Pennsylvania State University. Enrollment (1971): 38,448 at University Park, 22,653 at Commonwealth Campuses, Delaware County; Ogontz Campus. These are two of nineteen Commonwealth Campuses which exist in addition to the main campus at University Park. The Commonwealth Campuses offer two-year, undergraduate programs with transfer credit or an Associate degree. They are coeducational and have no residential facilities.

Rosemont College. Enrollment (1972): 600 women. Rosemont is a private, liberal arts, Catholic school. Founded in 1921, it is located in a suburban area. It has an undergraduate program offering the B.A. and B.F.A.

St. Joseph's College. Enrollment (1972): 1650 men, 350 women. This is a private, liberal arts, Catholic institution. Founded in 1851, it is located in residential Philadelphia. Most of its students are day students. It has an undergraduate program and a graduate program in chemistry; the undergraduate program offers the A.B. and B.S.

Swarthmore College. Enrollment (1972): 659 men, 490 women. Swarthmore is a private, liberal arts and engineering school, established by the Society of Friends. Founded in 1864, it has a suburban campus. The program is undergraduate only, offering the B.A. and B.S.

Temple University. Enrollment (1972): 7251 men, 5077 women (additional part-time and special students bring the estimate to 33,000 students in all its programs). One of the largest universities in the country, Temple became a state-related institution in 1965. The university has several campuses, one of them suburban, and seventeen schools and colleges. Founded in 1884, its main location is in north-central Philadelphia. It offers graduate and undergraduate programs; undergraduate programs lead to the B.A., B.S., B. Bus. Ad., B.S. Ed., and B. Mus.

University of Pennsylvania. Enrollment (1972): 4947 men, 2273 women. A private, state-aided, nonsectarian institution, the University of Pennsylvania was the first educational institution in the United States to be called a "university." Founded by Benjamin Franklin in 1740, it is an urban school located in West Philadelphia. It offers graduate and undergraduate programs in eighteen schools; the undergraduate programs lead to the B.A. or B.S.

Ursinus College. Enrollment (1972): 617 men, 517 women. A private, liberal arts school affiliated with the United Church of Christ, Ursinus is located in a small town about 25 miles northwest of Philadelphia. Founded in 1869, it has an undergraduate program which offers the B.A. and B.S.

Villanova University. Enrollment (1972): 4721 men, 1089 women. Villanova is a private, Catholic institution. Founded in 1842, it is located in a suburban community west of Philadelphia. It offers graduate and undergraduate programs; undergraduate programs lead to the B.A., B.S., B.Ch. E., B.C.E., B.E.E., and B.M.E.

West Chester State College. Enrollment (1972): 2202 men, 3459 women. This is a state-owned, liberal arts institution oriented to teacher training. Like Cheyney, it formerly was a State Teachers College. Founded in 1812, it is located in a community 27 miles west of Philadelphia. It offers undergraduate and graduate programs; undergraduate programs lead to the B A., B.S., and B.S. Ed.

Widener College. Enrollment (1972): 1294 men, 234 women. Widener College (formerly PMC College) was formed through the merger of a military school for men and a small, private, coeducational, liberal arts school. Its campus is located in the small city of Chester, south of Philadelphia. It offers graduate and undergraduate programs; undergraduate programs lead to the B.A., B.S., BS.S.B.A., B.S. in Engineering, and B.S.N.

Special, Technical, and Professional

Delaware Valley College of Science and Agriculture. Enrollment (1972): 950 men, 33 women. This is a private, state-aided, nonsectarian school offering scientific education in the specialized fields of agriculture, science, and business administration. Founded in 1896, it has a rural campus located in Bucks County north of Philadelphia. It has an undergraduate program offering the B.S.

Dropsie University. This is a graduate institution, founded in 1907 as Dropsie College for Hebrew and Cognate Learning. Nontheological, nonsectarian, and coeducational, it is oriented to studies of the ancient and modern cultures of the Middle East. It is located in north-central Philadelphia.

Eastern Baptist Theological Seminary. Enrollment (1971): 198. This institution is a coeducational theological seminary located in residential Philadelphia.

Gratz College. Enrollment (1972): 145 men, 216 women. Gratz College is the oldest Hebrew Teachers College in the Western hemisphere. Founded in 1895, it is located in Philadelphia. It has an undergraduate program which offers the B. Hebrew Literature and B. Religious Education.

Hahnemann Medical College and Hospital. Enrollment (1970): 477. This is a private, state-aided institution. Founded in 1848, it is located in center-city Philadelphia. In addition to the M.D., it offers the M.S., Ph.D., and other programs in medical technology.

Medical College of Pennsylvania. Enrollment (1971). 411. Formerly Womens Medical College, this is a private, state-aided institution in urban Philadelphia. Originally established in 1850 to provide medical education for women, it is now coeducational. It offers the M.D.

Moore College of Art. Enrollment (1972): 560 women. This is a private professional school of art. Founded in 1844, it is located in central Philadelphia and is the oldest professional art college for women. Its undergraduate program offers the B.F.A. and B.S. in Art. Ed.

Philadelphia College of Art. Enrollment (1972): 484 men, 531 women. This is a private, state-aided professional school of art and design. Founded in 1876 as part of the Philadelphia Museum of Art, it is located in central Philadelphia. It has graduate and undergraduate programs; its undergraduate program offers the B.F.A. and B.S.

Philadelphia College of Bible. Enrollment (1972): 309 men, 319 women. This is a private, nonsectarian professional school for Christian vocations. Founded in 1913, it is located in central Philadelphia. Its undergraduate program offers the B.S. and B. Mus.

Philadelphia College of Optometry. Enrollment (1971): 452. This is a private, state-aided, professional institution. It was founded in 1919 and is located in Philadelphia. It offers coeducational graduate and undergraduate programs leading to the B.S. and Dr. of Optometry.

Philadelphia College of Osteopathic Medicine.   Enrollment (1971): 575. This is a private, state-aided, coeducational institution. It is located in Philadelphia and was established in 1898.

Philadelphia College of Pharmacy and Science.   Enrollment (1972): 632 men, 259 women. This is a private, professional school. Founded in 1821, it has an urban campus. It offers graduate and undergraduate programs; graduate programs lead to the Dr. of Pharmacy, M.S., and Ph.D., undergraduate programs lead to the B.S. and B.S. in Pharmacy.

Philadelphia College of Podiatric Medicine.   Founded in 1963, this professional school awards the degree of Dr. of Podiatric Medicine at the completion of a four-year course. It has a central Philadelphia campus. It offers graduate programs only.

Philadelphia College of Textiles and Science.   Enrollment (1972): 1000 men, 250 women. This is a private, state-aided, nonsectarian, technological institution. Established in 1884 by the Pennsylvania Manufacturers Association, it is located in residential Philadelphia. It has an undergraduate program offering the B.S.

Philadelphia Divinity School.   Enrollment: 65. This is a Protestant Episcopal theological seminary, located in west Philadelphia. It is coeducational and offers a graduate program leading to the M.Div.

Philadelphia Musical Academy.   Enrollment (1972): 160 men, 85 women. This is a private, state-aided, college of music. Founded in 1870, it is located in central Philadelphia. It offers, in an undergraduate program, the B.Mus. and B.Mus.-B.Mus.Ed.

St. Charles Borromeo Seminary. Enrollment (1972): 130 men. This is a Catholic liberal arts and theological school for men preparing for the priesthood. Founded in 1832, it is located in urban Philadelphia. It offers the B.A. in philosophy and B.Div.

Spring Garden College. Enrollment (1972): 772 men, 30 women. This is a private, nonsectarian institution offering programs in technology and science. Founded in 1851 as Spring Garden Institute, it is located in residential Philadelphia. It offers undergraduate and continuing education programs leading to the B.S. in Technology and Associate in Science.

Thomas Jefferson University. Enrollment (1971): 1580. Formerly Jefferson Medical School, this is a private, state-aided, coeducational institution. Founded in 1824, it is located in central Philadelphia. It includes the Medical College, College of Allied Health Sciences, College of Graduate Studies, and the University Hospital.

Westminster Seminary. Enrollment (1969): 120. This is a private theological seminary of the Presbyterian adherence. It has a suburban campus, and offers both undergraduate and graduate programs.

Community Colleges

Community College of Philadelphia. Enrollment (1971): 5963.

Bucks County Community College. Enrollment (1971): 5162.

Delaware County Community College. Enrollment (1971): 2606.

Montgomery County Community College. Enrollment (1971): 3326.

The Community College of Philadelphia is located in central Philadelphia. The others have rural settings in their respective counties. All offer post-high school vocational programs, continuing education programs, and two-year academic transfer programs. Financial support comes from the state, the participating school districts, and the students.

Junior Colleges

Ellen Cushing Junior College.   This private institution for women is located in the suburbs west of Philadelphia.

Harcum Junior College.   This private institution for women is located in the suburbs west of Philadelphia.

Manor Junior College.   This private institution for women is located in the suburbs north of Philadelphia.

North East Christian Junior College.   A coeducational school, this institution is located in the suburbs west of Philadelphia.

Peirce Junior College.   A coeducational institution, the school is located in Philadelphia although a move to a suburban location is being planned.

Valley Forge Military Junior College.   This is a military school for men located in the western suburbs of Philadelphia.

NEW JERSEY

General

Glassboro State College. Enrollment (1972): 2800 men, 3300 women. This is a state-supported liberal arts school oriented toward teacher education. Founded in 1923, its campus is located in a small town. It offers undergraduate and graduate programs; the undergraduate program leads to the B.A.

Camden College of Arts and Sciences. Enrollment (1972): 1369 men, 870 women. This is a division of Rutgers, the state university. Located in Camden, it is a commuter college. It offers an undergraduate program and a graduate law school. The undergraduate program leads to the B.A. and B.S. in Med. Tech.

Community Colleges

Burlington County Community College.

Camden County Community College.

Gloucester County Community College.

These are publicly-supported institutions offering two-year programs in vocational fields and continuing education and academic transfer programs.

Index

Ackoff, Russell L., 54–55
Adelphi University, 70
Adult Leadership Training
 Program, 53
Albee, G. W., 172
*Autobiography of Malcolm
 X,* 92

Bacon, Edmund, 33
Bard, M., 146
Barnett, H. G., 102
Beaver College, 31, 197
Beck, B., 70
Beckett New Town, N.J.,
 63–64
Benne, K. D., 170
Bennis, Warren G., 19–27,
 180
Berkowitz, B., 146
Biddle, W. W., 73
Blumberg, L., 124
Blumer, H., 185
Bourne, P., 187
Brautigan, Richard, 20–21
Bronfenbrenner, U.,
 130
Brooke, Edward W., 92
Bruyn, S. T., 73
Bryn Mawr College, 31,
 197
Bucks County Community
 College, 204

Burlington County
 Community College, 206

Cabrini College, 197
Cahill, Edward E., 69–86
Camden College of Arts and
 Sciences, 206
Camden County Community
 College, 206
Carnegie Commission on
 Higher Education, 113
Case Institute, 70
Cheney, Edward Potts, 35
Chermayeff, S., 33–34
Chestnut Hill College, 197
Cheyney State College, 197
Chicago, University of,
 School of Social Work, 70
Cincinnati, University of,
 19–27
Clark, Joseph S., 33
Cleaver, Eldridge, 92
Cloward, R. A., 70, 123
Coleman, John R., 31, 32,
 107–120
College of Agriculture, 128,
 129, 133
Community College of
 Philadelphia, 204
Community development
 evolution, 122–124

207